Holiday Cheer

Holiday Cheer

Festive Inspirations for Your Best Season Ever!

HEARST BOOKS
New York

Contents

Cookie Cookbook

43
Give your tree personality!

All Through the House

15
Easy-Bake Favorites

Presents to Make and Bake

Christmas Dinners

Holiday Desserts

Cookie
Cookbook

Who isn't sweet on these delightful holiday treats?
From Linzer cookies to snowflakes to gingerbread men and more,
our recipes are a pleasure to bake, give—and eat!

On wire rack: Whole-Grain
Gingersnaps, Best Linzer
Cookies, and Brownie Bites.
Top: Lemon Meringue Drops.

Yes, Healthy Cookies!

If you don't like the flavor and texture of whole wheat, try white whole wheat flour instead. Milled from an albino variety of wheat, it's as healthy as the traditional kind—with the same levels of fiber, nutrients, and minerals—but lacks the heartier taste and grainy heft. It's ideal for all whole-grain recipes and can be substituted for up to half the all-purpose flour in many other recipes without changing the taste.

Chocoholics Only!

Brownie Bites can be topped with a peppermint icing (see photo on previous page) or fudge frosting. It's your choice!

Whole-Grain Gingersnaps

From Good Housekeeping
Prep 45 minutes plus chilling
Cook 9 minutes per batch
Makes 7 dozen cookies

- 2 cups all-purpose flour
- 2 cups whole wheat flour
- 2 Tbsp. ground ginger
- 2 tsp. baking soda
- 1 tsp. ground cinnamon
- 1 tsp. salt
- 1 cup sugar
- ¾ cup trans-fat free vegetable oil spread (60 to 70% oil)
- 2 large eggs
- 1 cup dark molasses
  Nonpareils or round white sprinkles (optional)

1. In medium bowl, whisk all-purpose and whole wheat flours, ground ginger, baking soda, cinnamon, and salt until blended. In large bowl, with mixer on low speed, beat sugar and oil spread until blended. On high speed, beat until light and creamy, scraping bowl with rubber spatula. Beat in eggs and molasses. On low speed, blend in flour mixture. Cover dough and refrigerate until easier to handle (dough will be sticky), 1 hour.

2. Preheat oven to 350°F. With well-greased hands, shape dough into 1-inch balls. Dip tops of balls in nonpareils; place 2½ inches apart on ungreased cookie sheets.

3. Bake cookies until tops are slightly cracked, 9 to 11 minutes. (Cookies will be very soft.) Cool cookies on cookie sheets for 1 minute. With metal spatula, transfer cookies to wire rack to continue cooling. Repeat process with remaining dough. Cookies may be stored in airtight container at room temperature up to 3 days or in freezer up to 1 month.

Make Linzer Cookies using stars, circles, or any other cutter shape you like.

Best Linzer Cookies

From Good Housekeeping
Prep 2 hours plus chilling
Cook 17 minutes per batch
Makes 8 dozen cookies

- 2 bags (8 oz. each) pecans
- 1 cup cornstarch
- 3 cups butter (6 sticks), softened (no substitutions)
- 2⅔ cups confectioners' sugar
- 4 tsp. vanilla extract
- 1½ tsp. salt
- 2 large eggs
- 5½ cups all-purpose flour
- 1½ cups seedless raspberry jam

1. In food processor with knife blade attached, pulse pecans and cornstarch until pecans are finely ground.

2. In large bowl, with mixer at low speed, beat butter and 2 cups confectioners' sugar until blended. Increase speed to high; beat until light and fluffy, about 3 minutes. At medium speed, beat in vanilla, salt, and eggs. On low speed, beat in flour and pecan mixture just until blended.

3. Divide dough into 8 equal pieces; flatten each into a disk and wrap in plastic. Refrigerate until dough is firm enough to roll, 4 to 5 hours.

4. Preheat oven to 325°F. Remove 1 disk of dough from refrigerator; let stand 5 minutes. On floured surface, with floured rolling pin, roll dough ⅛-inch thick. With floured 2¼-inch fluted square cookie cutter, cut dough into cookies. With floured 1¾-inch star cutter, cut out centers from half of cookies. With spatula, place cookies, 1 inch apart, on ungreased cookie sheets. Refrigerate trimmings.

5. Bake cookies until edges are golden, 17 to 20 minutes. Transfer to wire rack to cool. Repeat with remaining dough and trimmings.

6. Sprinkle remaining ⅔ cup confectioners' sugar through sieve over cooled cookies with cut-out centers.

7. Spread each whole cookie with scant teaspoon jam; top with cut-out cookies. Store in tightly sealed container, with waxed paper between layers, at room temperature up to 1 week or in freezer up to 2 months. (If cookies are frozen, re-sprinkle with confectioners' sugar before serving.)

Brownie Bites

From Good Housekeeping
Prep 35 minutes plus cooling
Cook 7 minutes per batch
Makes 2 dozen cookies

NOTE: Choose either the Peppermint Topping or the Fudge Frosting below.

BROWNIE BITES
- ⅔ cup all-purpose flour
- ½ cup unsweetened cocoa powder
- ½ tsp. baking powder
  Pinch of salt
- ¾ cup granulated sugar
- 3 Tbsp. butter or margarine, melted and cooled
- 2 Tbsp. honey
- 1 tsp. vanilla extract
- 1 large egg white

PEPPERMINT TOPPING
- 1 cup confectioners' sugar
- 1 Tbsp. milk
- 1 Tbsp. butter or margarine, softened
- ½ tsp. peppermint extract
- 2 oz. white chocolate, melted and cooled
- 2 oz. round hard peppermint candies, broken into chunks

FUDGE FROSTING
- 1 oz. unsweetened chocolate, coarsely chopped
- 3 Tbsp. water
- 1 tsp. trans-fat free vegetable oil spread (60 to 70% oil)
- ½ tsp. vanilla extract
- ⅔ cup confectioners' sugar

1. BROWNIE BITES: Preheat oven to 350°F. Grease large cookie sheet.

2. In large bowl, combine flour, cocoa, baking powder, and salt. In medium bowl, whisk sugar, butter, honey, vanilla, and egg white until blended. Stir sugar mixture into flour mixture; then, with hand, press dough just until blended.

3. With greased hands, shape dough into 1-inch balls and place on prepared cookie sheet 2 inches apart; press to flatten slightly. Bake brownies 7 to 8 minutes or until tops have cracked slightly. Transfer to wire rack to cool.

PEPPERMINT TOPPING: In medium bowl, whisk confectioners' sugar and milk until smooth. Whisk in butter and extract, then whisk in melted chocolate until smooth. Swirl 1 tsp. topping on each cookie. Top each frosted cookie with 1 candy piece. Store in tightly sealed container, with waxed paper between layers, at room temperature up to 3 days or in freezer up to 1 month.

FUDGE FROSTING: In microwave-safe small bowl, heat chocolate and water in microwave oven on High 45 seconds; stir until smooth. Stir in vegetable oil spread, then vanilla and confectioners' sugar. Cool slightly. Dip top of each cookie in frosting. Set aside to allow frosting to dry. Store brownies in tightly covered container, with waxed paper between layers, at room temperature up to 3 days or in freezer up to 1 month.

Cookie-Cutter Classics

Sugar Cookies

From Good Housekeeping
Prep 1 hour 30 minutes
Cook 12 minutes per batch
Makes 12½ dozen cookies

- 6 **cups all-purpose flour**
- 1 **tsp. baking powder**
- 1 **tsp. salt**
- 2 **cups butter (4 sticks), softened (no substitutions)**
- 3 **cups sugar**
- 4 **large eggs**
- 2 **tsp. vanilla extract**
  Ornamental Frosting (at right)

1. In large bowl, whisk flour, baking powder, and salt. In another large bowl, with mixer at low speed, beat butter and sugar until blended. On high speed, beat until light and fluffy, about 5 minutes. On low speed, beat in eggs and vanilla, then flour mixture just until blended, scraping bowl with rubber spatula.

2. Divide dough into 8 equal pieces; flatten each into a disk; wrap in plastic wrap and refrigerate overnight.

3. Preheat oven to 350°F. On floured surface, with floured rolling pin, roll 1 piece of dough to scant ¼-inch thickness; keep remaining dough cold. With floured 3- to 4-inch cookie cutters, cut dough into as many cookies as possible; reserve trimmings. Place cookies, 1 inch apart, on ungreased cookie sheets.

4. Bake cookies until edges are golden, 12 to 15 minutes. With wide metal spatula, transfer cookies to wire racks to cool. Repeat with remaining dough and trimmings.

5. When cookies are cool, prepare Ornamental Frosting (below); use to decorate cookies. Allow frosting to dry, about 1 hour. Store cookies in tightly sealed containers, with waxed paper between layers, at room temperature up to 2 weeks or in freezer up to 3 months.

Ornamental Frosting

Prep 6 minutes
Makes 3 cups

NOTE: Buy meringue powder wherever cake-decorating supplies are sold, or you can order it online at wilton.com.

- 1 **package (16 oz.) confectioners' sugar**
- 3 **Tbsp. meringue powder**
- ⅓ **cup warm water**
  Assorted food colorings

1. In bowl, with mixer at medium speed, beat confectioners' sugar, meringue powder, and water until blended and mixture is so stiff that knife drawn through it leaves a clean-cut path, about 5 minutes.

2. Tint frosting with food colorings as desired; keep surface covered with plastic to prevent drying out.

Gear Up!
For Better Baking...

Make sure your kitchen is ready for another busy holiday season with these top-of-the-line tools.

● KitchenAid Cook's Series Nonstick Rolling Pin. With this rolling pin, all you need is a light sprinkling of flour. (It's coated with a material similar to the one on nonstick pans.)

● Wilton Non-stick Mini Holiday Pan. Press cookie dough into 12 holiday-shaped molds built right into this nonstick baking sheet. The finished cookies pop right out.

An Easy Way to Make It Merry

Zip-seal bags can be used to pipe Ornamental Frosting on holiday cookies, or drizzle melted chocolate on desserts for a festive garnish. Add icing or chocolate to bag; cut a small opening in one corner and gently squeeze.

Christmas Balls

The word *dragée* (pronounced "dra-zhay") is French, meaning "to dredge." It traditionally refers to a colorful covered candy with a hard outer shell and a softer center. Dragées are an eye-catching, edible decoration.

Sugar & Spice Snowflakes

From Redbook **Prep** 20 minutes **Chill** 2 hours
Cook 10 minutes per batch **Makes** about 4½ dozen cookies

- 3½ **cups all-purpose flour**
- 2 **tsp. ground cinnamon**
- 1½ **tsp. ground ginger**
- ½ **tsp. baking soda**
- ½ **tsp. salt**
- ¼ **tsp. ground cloves**
- ¼ **tsp. ground nutmeg**
- 1 **cup (2 sticks) unsalted butter, softened**
- ¾ **cup packed dark brown sugar**
- ½ **cup granulated sugar**
- 2 **large eggs**
  Ornamental Frosting (page 10)

1. In medium bowl, whisk flour, cinnamon, ginger, baking soda, salt, cloves, and nutmeg; in large bowl, beat butter and sugars until creamy. Beat in eggs one at a time. With a mixer on low speed, beat in flour mixture, one-half at a time, until blended. Divide dough into thirds; wrap each third in plastic wrap and press into a disk shape. Refrigerate until firm enough to roll, about 2 hours.

2. Preheat oven to 350°F. Lightly grease several large baking sheets. Roll 1 piece of dough at a time, on a lightly floured surface with a floured rolling pin, to scant ¼-inch thickness. With 3- to 4-inch snowflake cookie cutters, cut out cookies. Using the end of a drinking straw, cut out a small circle in each snowflake so cookies can be hung. Place 2 inches apart on prepared baking sheets. Bake 8 to 10 minutes, or until cookies are lightly browned at edges. Remove to wire racks to cool. Decorate cookies using Ornamental Frosting. Thread ribbon through holes to hang snowflakes.

Ice Like a Pro

Pssst! Want to know the secret to decorating cookies as beautiful as the ones here?

Top food stylist Sara Neumeier is the creative genius behind some of our irresistible treats. Here are instructions for decorating the adorable Christmas tree cookie below:

- First make the **Ornamental Frosting** recipe on page 10. Reserve half for piping and thin the other half with 1 tsp. **water** at a time until a knife drawn through the icing leaves a clear-cut path that takes 7 seconds to disappear.
- Reserve a small amount of the thinned frosting and add **green food coloring** to the rest. Frost the cookies with the green frosting and, while it is still wet, place drops of the thinned white frosting on the cookies using a dessert bag fitted with a Number 2 pastry tip. Then pull a toothpick through the drops to form hearts.
- Repeat in the pattern shown below. When frosting on the cookies is dry, add **red food coloring** to the reserved frosting and, using a dessert bag fitted with a Number 2 pastry tip, pipe on red dots.

Lemon Sugar Cookies From Redbook

Prep 35 minutes **Chill** 2 hours **Cook** 10 minutes per batch **Makes** about 6 dozen cookies

1½ cups (3 sticks) unsalted
  butter, softened
1 cup sugar
1 large egg
2½ tsp. lemon extract
1 tsp. vanilla extract
½ tsp. salt
4 cups all-purpose flour
  Ornamental Frosting (page 10)

1. In a large bowl, beat butter and sugar until fluffy. Beat in egg, lemon and vanilla extracts, and salt. With a mixer on low speed, beat in flour in 2 additions until blended. Divide dough into thirds; shape each into a disk and wrap in plastic wrap. Refrigerate until firm enough to roll, about 2 hours.

2. Preheat oven to 350°F. Roll 1 piece of dough at a time, on a lightly floured surface with a floured rolling pin, to ¼-inch thickness. Cut out desired shapes with cookie cutters; re-roll scraps. Place 1½ inches apart on ungreased cookie sheets. Bake 8 to 10 minutes, or until golden. Cool on wire racks. Decorate as you like using Ornamental Frosting.

One Dough 12 Ways

Smart cookies are strategic about their holiday baking. If you want to whip up
a diverse assortment of goodies in record time, then we'll let you in a flour-power secret:
Use one do-it-all dough, like the triple-tested version below. It's quick to make and can turn
out 12 types of delicious—and distinctive—cookies, including fruit bars, rugelach, and
thumbprints. One thing's for sure: They'll all hit the sweet spot with family and friends.

This simple dough, which is the starting point for the 12 recipes that follow, calls for butter (no substitutions) for two reasons. One: Butter gives the best flavor in baked goods. Two: Margarines and spreads are often too soft to produce a cookie that can be rolled or shaped with ease.

Basic Cookie Dough
From Good Housekeeping
Prep 10 minutes

2¾ cups all-purpose flour
¼ tsp. baking soda
¼ tsp. salt
1 cup (2 sticks) butter (no substitutions), softened
¾ cup granulated sugar
1 large egg
1 tsp. vanilla extract

1. On waxed paper, combine flour, baking soda, and salt.

2. In large bowl, with mixer on medium speed, beat butter and sugar 1 minute or until creamy, occasionally scraping bowl with rubber spatula. Add egg and vanilla; beat until well mixed. Reduce speed to low; gradually beat in flour mixture just until blended, occasionally scraping bowl.

3. Follow directions to make your choice of cookie.

FIG-FILLED MOONS

CHOCOLATE PINWHEELS

CHEWY FRUIT BARS

HAZELNUT CHOCOLATE
SANDWICH COOKIES

BUTTER COOKIE CUTOUTS

CRANBERRY-ORANGE
SPICE COOKIES

APPLE PIE SPICE RUGELACH

GINGERBREAD CUTOUTS

MEXICAN WEDDING
COOKIES

CHOCOLATE-DIPPED
PEPPERMINT STICKS

CHOCOLATE RASPBERRY
THUMBPRINTS

STAINED GLASS
ORNAMENTS

Fig-Filled Moons

Creating these
yuletide yummies couldn't
be easier with our step-by-step
instructions for tweaking the basic
seven-ingredient recipe (page 14).
For some cookies, you'll add extras like
dried fruit and chocolate chips. Others,
like the Butter Cookie Cutouts (page 20),
are even simpler. You keep the dough as
is, then embellish with icing and sugar
crystals. And let the kids help! There's
nothing cuter than a little one's
tiny finger indentation in the
Chocolate Raspberry Thumbprints (page 18).

Chewy Fruit Bars

Cranberry-Orange Spice Cookies

With our simple dough recipe and the dozen scrumptious variations that follow, you can make a different batch of cookies for every one of the 12 days of Christmas. Start your mixer!

Fig-Filled Moons

From Good Housekeeping
Prep 1½ hours plus chilling and cooling
Cook 12 minutes per batch
Makes 4 dozen cookies

    Basic Cookie Dough (page 14)
1 **large orange**
5 **oz. dried Mission figs , stems removed (about 1 cup)**
½ **cup walnuts**
¼ **cup raisins**
¼ **cup honey**
1½ **tsp. ground cinnamon**
1 **large egg, lightly beaten**

1. Prepare Basic Cookie Dough. Divide dough into 3 pieces. Flatten each piece into a disk; wrap each in plastic wrap. Refrigerate dough at least 2 hours or overnight, until firm enough to roll.

2. Meanwhile, grate ½ tsp. orange peel and squeeze 3 Tbsp. juice. In food processor with knife blade attached, combine orange peel and juice, figs, walnuts, raisins, honey, and cinnamon. Pulse until fig mixture is well blended with a coarse texture. Cover and set aside.

3. Preheat oven to 350°F. Between 2 sheets of waxed paper, roll 1 disk of dough ⅛ inch thick. Remove top sheet of waxed paper. With floured 2½-inch scalloped round biscuit or cookie cutter, cut out as many cookies as possible. Wrap and refrigerate trimmings to reroll later.

4. With spatula, carefully place cookies, 1 inch apart, on ungreased large cookie sheet. Spoon 1 level measuring teaspoon fig filling onto center of each cookie. Fold each cookie in half over filling; brush with egg. (If dough becomes too soft to work with at any time, place in freezer 10 to 15 minutes to firm up.)

5. Bake cookies 12 to 15 minutes or until tops are golden-brown. Transfer to wire rack to cool. Repeat with

remaining dough, dough trimmings, fig filling, and egg.

6. Store in tightly sealed container at room temperature up to 1 week or in freezer up to 3 months.

Cranberry-Orange Spice Cookies

From Good Housekeeping
Prep 40 minutes plus freezing and cooling
Cook 14 minutes per batch
Makes 5 dozen cookies

    Basic Cookie Dough (page 14)
½ **cup dried cranberries, finely chopped**
¼ **cup crystallized ginger, finely chopped**
2 **tsp. grated fresh orange peel**
1 **tsp. pumpkin pie spice**
3 **Tbsp. green sugar crystals**
3 **Tbsp. red sugar crystals**

1. Prepare Basic Cookie Dough. In step 2, stir in cranberries, ginger, orange peel, and pumpkin pie spice along with flour until well mixed. Divide dough in half.

2. On lightly floured surface, with hands, shape each half into 10-inch-long log. Using hands or 2 clean rulers on sides, press each log into 10-inch-long squared-off log. Wrap each in plastic wrap and freeze until firm enough to slice, 2 hours, or refrigerate overnight. (Logs can be frozen up to 1 month.)

3. Preheat oven to 350°F. On 1 sheet of waxed paper, place green sugar. Unwrap 1 log and press sides in sugar to coat. Cut log into ¼-inch-thick slices. Place slices, 1 inch apart, on ungreased large cookie sheet. Bake cookies 14 to 16 minutes or until golden. Transfer cookies to wire rack to cool. Repeat with red sugar and second log.

4. Store in tightly sealed container at room temperature up to 1 week or in freezer up to 3 months.

Chewy Fruit Bars

From Good Housekeeping
Prep 20 minutes plus cooling
Cook 25 minutes
Makes 4 dozen cookies

    Basic Cookie Dough (page 14)
¾ **tsp. baking soda**
1 **tsp. ground cinnamon**
1½ **cups packed dark brown sugar**
2 **large eggs**
1 **cup walnuts, chopped**
1 **cup pitted dried dates, chopped**
1 **cup dried tart cherries**
½ **cup dried apricot halves, chopped**
½ **cup golden raisins**
    Confectioners' sugar for dusting (optional)

1. Preheat oven to 350°F. Line 15½- by 10½-inch jelly-roll pan with foil, extending foil 2 inches above pan at ends; grease foil.

2. Prepare Basic Cookie Dough, but in step 1, decrease flour to 2½ cups, increase baking soda to ¾ tsp. total, and add cinnamon to flour mixture. In step 2, substitute 1½ cups packed dark brown sugar for granulated sugar and use a total of 2 eggs. Add walnuts, dates, cherries, apricots, and raisins to dough, stirring until blended.

3. With floured fingers, press dough evenly into prepared pan. Bake 25 to 28 minutes or until browned and toothpick inserted in center comes out clean. Cool completely. Remove from pan, using foil, and place on cutting board. With long, sharp knife, cut lengthwise into 4 strips, then cut each strip crosswise into 12 bars.

4. Store bars in tightly sealed container, with waxed paper between layers, at room temperature up to 1 week or in freezer up to 3 months. Dust with confectioners' sugar, if desired.

Gingerbread Cutouts

From Good Housekeeping
Prep 1½ hours plus chilling and cooling
Cook 11 minutes per batch
Makes 5 dozen cookies

    Basic Cookie Dough (page 14)
½ tsp. baking soda
2 tsp. ground cinnamon
2 tsp. ground ginger
½ tsp. ground nutmeg
¼ tsp. ground cloves
¾ cup packed dark brown sugar
¼ cup dark molasses
    Ornamental Frosting (optional; page 10)
    Small red candies (optional)

1. Prepare Basic Cookie Dough, but in step 1, increase baking soda to ½ tsp. total and add spices to flour mixture. In step 2, reduce butter to 1 stick, substitute dark brown sugar for granulated sugar, and add molasses with egg and vanilla.

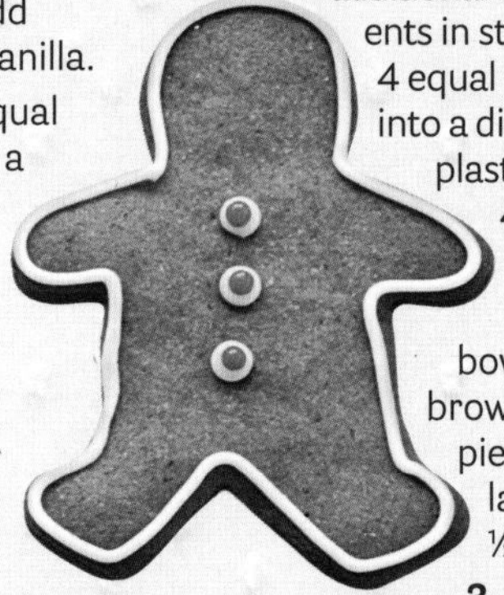

2. Divide dough into 3 equal pieces. Flatten each into a disk; wrap each in plastic wrap. Refrigerate dough 2 hours or overnight, until firm enough to roll.

3. Preheat oven to 350°F. Between 2 sheets of waxed paper, roll 1 disk of dough ⅛ inch thick. Remove top sheet of waxed paper. With floured 3- to 4-inch cookie cutters, cut out as many cookies as possible; wrap and refrigerate trimmings. Place cookies, 1 inch apart, on ungreased large cookie sheet.

4. Bake cookies 11 to 13 minutes or until edges begin to brown. Transfer cookies to wire rack to cool. Repeat with remaining dough and trimmings.

5. When cookies are cool, prepare Ornamental Frosting, if you like; add small red candies to decorate. as desired. Set cookies aside to allow frosting to dry, about 1 hour.

6. Store Gingerbread Cutouts in tightly sealed container (put waxed paper between layers if decorated) at room temperature up to 2 weeks or in freezer up to 3 months.

Apple Pie Spice Rugelach

From Good Housekeeping
Prep 1½ hours plus chilling and cooling
Cook 15 minutes per batch
Makes 4 dozen cookies

    Basic Cookie Dough (page 14)
⅓ cup all-purpose flour
1 cup dried currants
⅔ cup walnuts or pecans, finely chopped
¼ cup packed brown sugar
1½ tsp. apple pie spice
3 Tbsp. granulated sugar
½ cup plus 1 Tbsp. apple butter

1. Prepare Basic Cookie Dough, stirring additional ⅓ cup flour into dry ingredients in step 1. Divide dough into 4 equal pieces. Flatten each piece into a disk; wrap each disk with plastic wrap. Refrigerate dough 4 hours or overnight, until firm enough to roll.

2. Meanwhile, in small bowl, mix currants, walnuts, brown sugar, and 1 tsp. apple pie spice. In cup, mix granulated sugar with remaining ½ tsp. apple pie spice.

3. Preheat oven to 350°F. Between 2 sheets of waxed paper, roll 1 disk of dough into 9-inch round. Remove top sheet of waxed paper. Spread 1 heaping Tbsp. apple butter on dough; sprinkle with ½ cup fruit mixture, leaving ¼-inch border around edge.

4. With pizza wheel or sharp knife, cut round into 12 wedges. (If dough becomes too soft to work with, place in refrigerator 10 to 15 minutes to firm

up.) Starting at curved edge, roll up each wedge jelly-roll fashion. Place cookies, point side down, 1 inch apart, on ungreased large cookie sheet; shape into crescents. Brush tops lightly with water and sprinkle with some spiced sugar. Bake 15 minutes or until golden brown. Transfer cookies to wire rack to cool. Repeat with remaining dough, fruit mixture, and spiced sugar.

5. Store Apple Pie Spice Rugelach in tightly sealed container, with waxed paper between layers, at room temperature up to 2 weeks or in freezer up to 3 months.

Chocolate Raspberry Thumbprints

From Good Housekeeping
Prep 40 minutes plus cooling
Cook 14 minutes per batch
Makes 7 dozen cookies

    Basic Cookie Dough (page 14)
2 oz. unsweetened chocolate, melted
¼ cup unsweetened cocoa powder
1¼ cup sliced natural almonds, coarsely chopped
½ cup seedless red raspberry jam

1. Preheat oven to 350°F.

2. Prepare Basic Cookie Dough. In step 2, beat in chocolate and cocoa with egg and vanilla extract. With hands, shape dough by rounded measuring teaspoons into 1-inch balls. Place almonds on sheet of waxed paper; roll balls in chopped almonds to coat.

3. Place balls, 1½ inches apart, on ungreased large cookie sheet. With thumb, make small indentation in center of each; fill with ¼ tsp. jam. Bake cookies 14 to 15 minutes or until jam is bubbly and cookies are baked through. Transfer cookies to wire rack to cool. Repeat with remaining balls and jam.

4. Store Chocolate Raspberry Thumbprints in tightly sealed container, with waxed paper between layers, at room temperature up to 3 days or in freezer up to 3 months .

Chocolate Pinwheels

From Good Housekeeping
Prep 30 minutes plus freezing and cooling
Cook 10 minutes per batch
Makes 4 dozen cookies

Basic Cookie Dough (page 14)
⅓ cup miniature semisweet chocolate chips
¼ cup confectioners' sugar
1 oz. unsweetened chocolate, melted
2 Tbsp. unsweetened cocoa powder
2 Tbsp. all-purpose flour

1. Prepare Basic Cookie Dough. Transfer half to another bowl. Stir chips, sugar, chocolate, and cocoa powder into half. Stir flour into plain dough.

2. On sheet of waxed paper, roll chocolate dough into 14- by 10-inch rectangle. Repeat with plain dough. Turn over plain rectangle, still on waxed paper, and place, dough side down, on top of chocolate rectangle so that edges line up evenly. Peel off top sheet of waxed paper. If dough becomes too soft to work with, refrigerate 10 minutes. Starting from long side, tightly roll rectangles together, jelly-roll fashion, to form log, lifting bottom sheet of waxed paper to help roll. Cut log crosswise in half. Wrap each half with plastic wrap and freeze 2 hours or refrigerate overnight.

3. Preheat oven to 350°F. With sharp knife, cut 1 log (keep other log refrigerated) crosswise into ¼-inch-thick slices. Place slices, 2 inches apart, on ungreased large cookie sheet. Bake 10 minutes or until lightly browned. Transfer to wire racks to cool. Repeat with remaining log.

4. Store Pinwheels in tightly sealed container at room temperature up to 1 week or in freezer up to 3 months.

Chocolate-Dipped Peppermint Sticks

From Good Housekeeping
Prep 1 hour plus freezing and cooling
Cook 11 minutes per batch
Makes 5 dozen cookies

Basic Cookie Dough (page 14)
¼ tsp. peppermint extract
Green and red paste food coloring
5 oz. white chocolate, melted
6 green or red starlight mint candies, crushed

1. Prepare Basic Cookie Dough. Transfer half to another bowl. Stir peppermint extract into 1 portion of dough. Divide peppermint dough in half; transfer half to another bowl. Tint 1 portion green, the other red.

2. Preheat oven to 350°F. Line 9- by 9-inch metal baking pan with plastic wrap, extending wrap over 2 sides of pan. Pat plain dough in pan. Freeze 10 minutes. Pat green dough over half of plain dough; pat red dough over remaining plain dough. Freeze 10 minutes.

3. Lift dough from pan using plastic wrap; place on cutting board. Cut dough into thirds so that one-third is all red on top, one-third is all green on top, and middle third is half red and half green on top. Cut each third crosswise into ⅜-inch strips. Twist strips and place, 1½ inches apart, on ungreased cookie sheet. Bake 11 to 13 minutes or until golden-brown. Transfer to wire rack to cool. Repeat.

4. Dip 1 end of each cookie into chocolate and place on waxed paper. Sprinkle chocolate with crushed mints. Refrigerate 15 minutes to set.

5. Store Chocolate-Dipped Peppermint Sticks in tightly sealed container, with waxed paper between layers, at room temperature up to 1 week or in freezer up to 3 months.

Hazelnut Chocolate Sandwich Cookies

From Good Housekeeping
Prep 1½ hours plus cooling
Cook 9 minutes per batch
Makes 6 dozen sandwich cookies

Basic Cookie Dough (page 14)
Sugar
⅓ cup hazelnuts, toasted and chopped
¾ cup chocolate-hazelnut spread

1. Prepare Basic Cookie Dough.

2. Preheat oven to 350°F. With hands, shape ½ tsp. of dough into balls. Place cookies, 2 inches apart, on ungreased large cookie sheet. Dip bottom of flat-bottomed glass in sugar and use to press each ball into 1-inch round. Sprinkle half of the rounds with hazelnuts. Bake cookies 9 to 10 minutes or until edges are golden-brown. Transfer cookies to wire rack to cool. Repeat.

3. Assemble sandwich cookies: Spread flat sides of plain cookies with ½ tsp. chocolate-hazelnut spread. Top each with a nut-covered cookie, top side up, pressing lightly.

4. Store Hazelnut Chocolate Sandwich Cookies in tightly sealed container, with waxed paper between layers, at room temperature up to 1 week or in freezer up to 3 months.

Butter Cookie Cutouts

From Good Housekeeping
Prep 1½ hours plus chilling
and cooling
Cook 11 minutes per batch
Makes 5 dozen cookies

Basic Cookie Dough (page 14)
Colored sugar crystals (optional)
**Ornamental Frosting
(optional; page 10)**

1. Prepare Basic Cookie Dough; divide
into 3 equal pieces. Flatten each piece
into a disk, and wrap each in plastic
wrap. Refrigerate at least 2 hours or
overnight, until firm enough to roll.

2. Preheat oven to 350°F. Between
2 sheets of waxed paper, roll 1 disk of
dough ⅛ inch thick. Remove top sheet
of waxed paper. With floured 3- to
4-inch cookie cutters, cut dough into
as many cookies as possible; wrap and
refrigerate trimmings . Place cookies,
1 inch apart, on ungreased large
cookie sheet. Sprinkle with colored
sugar if you like.

3. Bake cookies 11 to 13 minutes or
until golden-brown. Transfer cookies
to wire rack to cool. Repeat with
remaining dough and trimmings.

4. When cookies are cool, prepare
Ornamental Frosting, if you like; use to
decorate cookies. Set cookies aside to
allow frosting to dry, about 1 hour.

5. Store cookies in tightly sealed
container (put waxed paper between
layers if decorated) at room temperature up to 2 weeks or in freezer up to
3 months.

Hang It Up

To use cookies as ornaments, poke a small hole in each unbaked cookie with a skewer. After baking and cooling, thread ribbon, string, or nylon fishing line through hole.

Stained Glass Ornaments

From Good Housekeeping **Prep** 1½ hours plus chilling and cooling
Cook 10 minutes per batch **Makes** 5 dozen cookies

Basic Cookie Dough (page 14)
1 **bag (6.25 oz.) hard candy, such as sour balls**

1. Prepare Basic Cookie Dough; divide into 3 pieces. Flatten each piece into a disk; wrap each in plastic wrap. Refrigerate at least 2 hours or overnight, until firm enough to roll.

2. While dough chills, place each color hard candy in separate heavy-duty plastic bag. Place 1 bag on towel-covered work surface or floor. With rolling pin, lightly crush candy into pieces about the size of coarsely chopped nuts.

3. Preheat oven to 350°F. Line large cookie sheet with foil. Between 2 sheets of waxed paper, roll 1 disk of dough ⅛ inch thick. Remove top sheet of waxed paper. With floured 3- to 4-inch cookie cutters, cut out cookies. Place cookies, 1 inch apart, on cookie sheet. Cut out centers of cookies with 1½- to 2-inch cookie cutters. Remove and refrigerate trimmings and cutout centers.

4. Bake cookies 7 minutes. Remove cookie sheet from oven; fill each cookie's center with ½ tsp. crushed candy. Return to oven and bake 3 to 4 minutes longer or until cookies are lightly browned and candy is melted. Cool cookies on cookie sheet on wire rack. With metal spatula, remove cookies. Repeat with remaining dough, trimmings, and candy.

5. Store cookies in tightly sealed container at room temperature up to 2 weeks or in freezer up to 3 months.

Mexican Wedding Cookies

From Good Housekeeping **Prep** 30 minutes plus cooling **Cook** 13 minutes per batch **Makes** 8 dozen cookies

1½ **cups pecans**
   Basic Cookie Dough
   (page 14)
 3 **Tbsp. plus 1½ cups**
   confectioners' sugar, sifted

1. In food processor with knife blade attached, pulse pecans with 3 Tbsp. confectioners' sugar until nuts are very finely ground.

2. Prepare Basic Cookie Dough, stirring ground pecans into flour mixture before adding to butter mixture in step 2.

3. Preheat oven to 350°F. Use a measuring teaspoon to shape dough into 1-inch balls. Place balls, 1½ inches apart, on ungreased large cookie sheet. Bake cookies 13 to 15 minutes or until bottoms are browned and cookies are light golden.

Let stand on cookie sheet 2 minutes, then transfer to wire rack to cool. Repeat with remaining dough.

4. Place confectioners' sugar in pie plate. Roll cooled cookies in sugar to coat, twice if desired .

5. Store Mexican Wedding Cookies, with waxed paper between layers, in tightly sealed container at room temperature up to 1 week or in freezer up to 3 months.

Sugar Smarts

Unlike similar recipes, this one calls for the cookies to be rolled in confectioners' sugar once they're cooled; if they're rolled while they're still warm, the coating will get sticky.

Macaroon Fingers

From Good Housekeeping
Prep about 30 minutes plus cooling
Cook about 17 minutes per batch
Makes about 3½ dozen cookies

- 1 **tube or can (7 to 8 oz.) almond paste**
- ½ **cup confectioners' sugar**
- 2 **large egg whites**
- ½ **tsp. vanilla extract**
- 2 **oz. bittersweet or semisweet chocolate, broken into pieces**

1. Preheat oven to 300°F. Line 2 cookie sheets with parchment.

2. In food processor with knife blade attached, process almond paste and sugar until combined. Add egg whites and vanilla; pulse until well combined.

3. Spoon batter into decorating bag fitted with ½-inch star tip. Pipe batter into 3-inch-long fingers, 1 inch apart, onto prepared cookie sheets.

4. Bake macaroons, on 2 oven racks, 17 to 19 minutes, rotating sheets between racks halfway through baking, until cookies start to turn golden brown on edges. Cool on cookie sheets on wire racks. Repeat.

5. Heat chocolate in microwave oven on High 1 minute or until soft and shiny. Remove; stir until smooth. With pastry brush, brush chocolate on half of each macaroon; let dry. Peel cookies from parchment; store tightly covered at room temperature, with waxed paper between layers, up to 3 days or in freezer up to 1 month.

Lighter Than Air

These melt-in-your-mouth meringues have only five calories each!

Lemon Meringue Drops

From Good Housekeeping **Prep** 45 minutes plus drying and cooling
Cook 1 hour 30 minutes per batch **Makes** about 10 dozen cookies

- 6 **large egg whites**
- ½ **tsp. cream of tartar**
- ¼ **tsp. salt**
- 1 **cup sugar**
- 4 **tsp. freshly grated lemon peel**

1. Preheat oven to 200°F. Line 2 large cookie sheets with parchment.

2. In medium bowl, with mixer at high speed, beat egg whites, cream of tartar, and salt until soft peaks form. With mixer running, sprinkle in sugar, 2 Tbsp. at a time, beating until sugar dissolves and meringue stands in stiff, glossy peaks when beaters are lifted. Gently fold in lemon peel.

3. Spoon meringue into decorating bag fitted with ½-inch star tip. Pipe meringue into 1½-inch stars, about 1 inch apart, on prepared cookie sheets.

4. Bake meringues until crisp but not brown, 1 hour 30 minutes, rotating cookie sheets between upper and lower racks halfway through baking. Turn oven off; leave meringues in oven until dry, 1 hour. Remove from oven. Turn oven temperature back to 200°F. Repeat with remaining meringue.

5. Cool meringues completely. Remove from parchment with wide metal spatula. Store in tightly sealed container at room temperature up to 1 month.

Chocolate Chip Jumbos

Peanut Butter Cookies

Ginger Cookies

Mix up a batch of one of these time-tested recipes. Perfected over generations, they're sure-to-delight sweets that will bring an old-fashioned flavor to your family's holidays.

Chocolate Chip Jumbos

From Good Housekeeping
Prep 40 minutes plus cooling
Cook about 23 minutes per batch
Makes about 3 dozen cookies

NOTE: Each of these great big treats is the equivalent of six regular chocolate chip cookies, so share the goodness!

- 3 large eggs
- 1 lb. butter or margarine (4 sticks), softened
- 1 package (16 oz.) brown sugar
- 1½ cups granulated sugar
- 2 Tbsp. vanilla extract
- 1½ tsp. baking soda
- 1½ tsp. salt
- 6 cups all-purpose flour
- 2 packages (12 oz. each) semisweet chocolate chips
- 1 bag (16 oz.) chopped walnuts

1. Preheat oven to 350°F. In very large bowl, with mixer on medium speed, beat eggs 4 minutes or until light and fluffy. Reduce speed to low; beat in butter, sugars, vanilla, baking soda, and salt. Stir in flour, chocolate chips, and walnuts (mixture will be very stiff).

2. Line 2 large cookie sheets with parchment paper. Drop dough by level ⅓ cups (or use 2½-inch ice cream scoop), 2 inches apart, onto prepared cookie sheets.

3. Bake cookies 23 to 26 minutes or until golden around the edges, rotating cookie sheets between upper and lower racks halfway through baking. Transfer cookies to wire racks to cool.

4. Repeat with remaining dough, reusing the same parchment. Store your cookies in a tightly covered container at room temperature for up to 1 week or in the freezer up to 3 months.

Peanut Butter Cookies

From Good Housekeeping
Prep 40 minutes plus cooling
Cook about 12 minutes per batch
Makes about 6 dozen cookies

- 2 cups all-purpose flour
- 1 tsp. baking powder
- 1 tsp. baking soda
- 1 tsp. salt
- 1 cup butter (2 sticks), softened (no substitutions)
- 1 cup packed brown sugar
- 1 cup plus 2 Tbsp. granulated sugar
- 1 tsp. vanilla extract
- 2 large eggs
- 1 jar (18 oz.) creamy peanut butter

1. Preheat oven to 350°F. On waxed paper, combine flour, baking powder, baking soda, and salt.

2. In large bowl, with mixer on medium speed, beat butter, brown sugar, and 1 cup granulated sugar 2 minutes or until creamy, occasionally scraping bowl with rubber spatula. Reduce speed to low; beat in vanilla, then eggs, one at a time, beating well after each addition. Add peanut butter, and beat on medium speed 2 minutes or until creamy. Reduce speed to low; beat in flour mixture just until blended, occasionally scraping bowl.

3. Drop dough by rounded measuring tablespoons, 2 inches apart, on ungreased large cookie sheet. Place remaining 2 Tbsp. granulated sugar on plate or sheet of waxed paper. Dip tines of fork in sugar, then press twice into top of each cookie, making a crisscross pattern.

4. Bake cookies 12 to 14 minutes or until lightly browned at edges. Cool cookies on cookie sheet 2 minutes. Transfer cookies to wire rack to cool completely. Repeat with remaining dough and sugar. Store cookies in tightly covered container at room temperature up to 2 weeks or in freezer up to 3 months.

Ginger Cookies

From Good Housekeeping
Prep 40 minutes plus cooling
Cook about 13 minutes per batch
Makes about 3½ dozen cookies

- ½ cup butter or margarine (1 stick)
- ¼ cup vegetable shortening
- 1 cup light molasses
- 1 Tbsp. baking soda
- 3½ cups all-purpose flour
- 1 cup sugar
- ½ cup buttermilk
- 1 Tbsp. ground ginger
- ¼ tsp. salt

1. Preheat oven to 350°F. Grease 2 large cookie sheets.

2. In small saucepan, heat butter and shortening over medium-low heat until melted, swirling pan occasionally.

3. In large bowl, whisk molasses and baking soda. Add butter mixture, flour, sugar, buttermilk, ginger, and salt, and stir until blended.

4. Drop dough by rounded measuring tablespoons, 3 inches apart, on prepared cookie sheets. Bake cookies 13 to 15 minutes, rotating cookie sheets between upper and lower racks halfway through baking.

5. Cool cookies on cookie sheets 1 minute, then with wide spatula, transfer to wire racks to cool completely. Repeat with remaining dough.

6. Store cookies in tightly covered container at room temperature up to 1 week or in freezer up to 3 months.

Holiday Oatmeal Cookies

From Good Housekeeping
Prep 40 minutes plus cooling
Cook 13 minutes per batch
Makes about 4 dozen cookies

- 1½ cups all-purpose flour
- 1 tsp. baking soda
- ½ tsp. salt
- 1 cup butter or margarine (2 sticks), softened
- ¾ cup packed brown sugar
- ½ cup granulated sugar
- 1 large egg
- 1 tsp. vanilla extract
- 3 cups old-fashioned oats, uncooked
- 1 cup raisins
- 1 package (6 oz.) semisweet chocolate chips (1 cup)

1. Preheat oven to 350°F.

2. On waxed paper, combine flour, baking soda, and salt. In large bowl, with mixer on medium speed, beat butter and sugars until creamy, occasionally scraping bowl with rubber spatula. Beat in egg and vanilla. Reduce speed to low; gradually beat in flour mixture just until blended, occasionally scraping bowl. With spoon, stir in oats, raisins, and chocolate chips.

3. Drop dough by heaping measuring tablespoons, 2 inches apart, on ungreased large cookie sheet. Bake cookies 13 to 15 minutes or until tops are golden. Transfer cookies to wire racks to cool.

Christmas Drops

From Redbook **Prep** 15 minutes
Cook 10 minutes per batch **Makes** about 3 dozen cookies

- 2½ cups all-purpose flour
- 1 tsp. baking soda
- 1 tsp. salt
- 1 cup (2 sticks) unsalted butter, softened
- ¾ cup granulated sugar
- ¾ cup packed brown sugar
- 2 large eggs
- 2 tsp. vanilla extract
- 1 cup white chocolate chips
- 1 cup semisweet or milk chocolate chips
- ½ cup red and green mini baking bits (M&M's mini baking bits)

1. Heat oven to 375°F. Line several baking sheets with parchment paper. In a bowl, whisk flour, baking soda, and salt.

2. In a large bowl, beat butter and sugars until light and fluffy. Beat in eggs and vanilla. Beat in flour mixture until blended. Stir in chocolate chips and baking bits.

3. Drop rounded tablespoons of dough, 3 inches apart, onto prepared baking sheets. Bake 9 to 10 minutes, or until cookies are browned at edges and no longer wet-looking in centers. Let stand on sheets for 2 minutes before removing to wire racks to cool.

Marzipan Bars From Redbook
Prep 35 minutes **Cook** 1 hour **Makes** about 3 dozen bars

CRUST
- 2½ cups all-purpose flour
- ¾ cup sugar
- ½ tsp salt
- 1 cup (2 sticks) cold unsalted butter, cut up
- 1 large egg, beaten

FILLING
- 1¼ cups sugar
- ¾ cup blanched almonds
- ¾ cup hazelnuts, toasted, skins removed
- ¼ cup all-purpose flour
- ½ cup (1 stick) unsalted butter, softened
- 3 large eggs
- 1 tsp. pure almond extract
- 1 tsp. vanilla extract
- 2 to 3 drops green food coloring, if desired

- ½ cup seedless raspberry jam
- 6 oz. bittersweet chocolate, chopped
- 2 tsp. vegetable shortening

1. CRUST: Preheat oven to 350°F. Line a 15½- by 10½-inch jelly-roll pan with foil, letting foil extend 2 inches at ends. In a food processor, pulse flour, sugar, and salt to combine. Add butter; pulse until mixture is the texture of coarse meal. Add egg and pulse until dough begins to hold together. Press dough evenly over bottom and sides of pan. Refrigerate 15 minutes. Bake 20 to 22 minutes, or until crust is browned at edges. Cool on rack while making filling.

2. FILLING: In food processor, process sugar, almonds, hazelnuts, and flour until nuts are very finely ground. Add butter and 1 egg. Process until smooth. Add remaining eggs, almond extract, vanilla extract, and green food coloring if using. Process until blended.

3. Spread jam over crust. Spoon filling over jam and spread to cover. Bake 30 to 35 minutes, until filling is golden brown and firm in center. Let cool on a wire rack.

4. Melt chocolate with shortening. Spread over filling. Refrigerate until chocolate sets. Carefully pull foil away from sides. Cut into squares.

Office Party
Crowd-
Pleaser

Looking for something different? Make a batch of these rich lemon butter-frosted tea cakes or chewy, chocolatey biscotti. They're a tempting twist on the usual holiday treats.

English Tea Cakes

From Good Housekeeping
Prep 30 minutes plus cooling
Cook about 48 minutes
Makes about 5 dozen cookies

TEA CAKES

- ¼ **cup confectioners' sugar**
- 1 **cup plus 2 Tbsp. all purpose flour**
- ½ **cup (1 stick) cold butter (no substitutions)**
- 2 **large eggs**
- 1½ **cups packed brown sugar**
- 1 **cup coarsely chopped pecans or walnuts**
- ½ **cup sweetened flaked coconut**
- 1 **tsp. vanilla extract**
- ½ **tsp. salt**
- ¼ **tsp. baking powder**

LEMON BUTTER FROSTING

- 1 **lemon**
- 1 **cup confectioners' sugar**
- 6 **Tbsp. butter, softened (no substitutions)**

1. Preheat oven to 350°F. Line 9- by 9-inch metal baking pan with foil, extending foil over ends.

2. TEA CAKES: In medium bowl, combine confectioners' sugar and 1 cup flour. With pastry blender or 2 knives used scissor-fashion, cut in butter until mixture resembles coarse crumbs. With fingertips, press mixture evenly onto bottom of prepared pan. Bake crust 23 to 25 minutes or until lightly browned. Remove from oven.

3. While crust bakes, in same medium bowl, with fork, mix eggs, brown sugar, nuts, coconut, vanilla, salt, baking powder, and remaining 2 Tbsp. flour until well blended. Spread topping evenly over hot crust. Return pan to oven; bake 25 minutes or until topping is just set and edges are golden. Cool completely in pan on wire rack.

4. LEMON BUTTER FROSTING: From

lemon, grate 1 tsp. peel and squeeze 4 tsp. juice. In bowl, with mixer on medium speed, beat lemon peel and juice with remaining frosting ingredients until smooth. Spread frosting over top of cake. Refrigerate 10 to 15 minutes to allow frosting to firm slightly for easier cutting.

5. Transfer tea cake with foil to cutting board. Carefully pull foil away from sides. Cut into 8 strips, then cut each strip crosswise into 8 bars.

6. Store cookies in tightly covered container, with waxed paper between layers, in refrigerator up to 1 week or in freezer up to 1 month.

Chocolate-Filled Biscotti

From Good Housekeeping
Prep 1 hour plus chilling overnight and cooling
Cook about 20 minutes per batch
Makes 8 dozen biscotti

CREAM CHEESE DOUGH

- 4 **cups all-purpose flour**
- 1 **tsp. baking powder**
- 1 **tsp. salt**
- 1 **cup butter (2 sticks), softened (no substitutions)**
- 6 **oz. cream cheese, softened**
- 1 **cup granulated sugar**
- 1 **cup packed brown sugar**
- 2 **large eggs**
- 1 **Tbsp. vanilla extract**

CHOCOLATE FILLING

- 1 **can (14 oz.) sweetened condensed milk**
- 8 **oz. bittersweet or semisweet chocolate, cut up**
- 1 **cup walnuts, coarsely chopped**
  Confectioners' sugar for sprinkling

1. CREAM CHEESE DOUGH: In medium bowl, combine flour, baking powder, and salt. In large bowl, with

mixer on medium speed, beat butter and cream cheese until well blended. Gradually add sugars, and beat 3 minutes. Add eggs, one at a time, beating well. Beat in vanilla. Reduce speed to low; gradually beat in flour mixture just until blended.

2. Place level ¾ cup dough on sheet of plastic wrap. Repeat to make 7 more ¾ cupfuls. Wrap each with plastic wrap and refrigerate overnight.

3. CHOCOLATE FILLING: When ready to roll out dough, prepare chocolate filling. In 2-quart saucepan, heat sweetened condensed milk and chocolate over medium heat just until chocolate melts, stirring frequently. Remove saucepan from heat; stir in walnuts. Let filling cool to room temperature.

4. Preheat oven to 350°F. Grease 2 large cookie sheets.

5. Remove 1 piece of dough from refrigerator. On lightly floured 16-inch sheet of waxed paper, with floured rolling pin, roll dough into 10- by 6-inch rectangle. Spread heaping ¼ cup filling lengthwise down center of rectangle. Starting from a long side and using waxed paper to help lift dough, fold 1 side of dough lengthwise over filling, then remaining side over dough (dough should overlap).

6. Pick up waxed paper and flip cookie log onto 1 side of prepared cookie sheet, seam side down. Repeat with another piece of dough and filling. Flip second log parallel to first log, leaving about 2 inches between logs.

7. Bake logs 20 to 22 minutes or until edges are lightly golden. Cool logs on cookie sheet 2 minutes, then transfer to wire rack to cool completely.

8. While logs bake, repeat with remaining dough and filling.

9. Wrap each cooled log separately with foil or plastic wrap, and store in tightly covered containers at room temperature up to 2 weeks or in freezer up to 3 months. To serve, sprinkle logs with confectioners' sugar. Cut each log crosswise on the diagonal into 12 slices.

Elegant Sweets

Plenty of chopped nuts and
brown sugar make
English Tea Cakes and
Chocolate-Filled Biscotti
especially delicious.

Have Cookies
Will Travel

It's sweet to send a batch of homemade cookies to a far-off friend or family member, but no one wants a box of pulverized crumbs. These tips will ensure your treats arrive intact.

Triple-Nut Biscotti From Good Housekeeping
Prep about 25 minutes plus cooling **Cook** about 50 minutes
Makes about 4 dozen biscotti

- ⅓ **cup whole natural almonds**
- ⅓ **cup shelled pistachios**
- ⅓ **cup walnuts**
- 1 **cup all-purpose flour**
- ⅔ **cup whole wheat flour**
- ⅔ **cup sugar**
- ¼ **cup toasted wheat germ**
- 1½ **tsp. baking powder**
- ½ **tsp. ground cinnamon**
- ¼ **tsp. salt**
- 2 **large egg whites**
- 1 **large egg**
- ¼ **cup water**
- ½ **tsp. grated fresh lemon peel**

1. Preheat oven to 325°F. Grease large cookie sheet; set aside.

2. In 13- by 9-inch metal baking pan, bake nuts until toasted, about 15 minutes, stirring once. Cool in pan on wire rack. Coarsely chop nuts.

3. In large bowl, stir nuts, flours, sugar, wheat germ, baking powder, cinnamon, and salt. In small bowl, beat egg whites, egg, water, and lemon peel. With wooden spoon, stir egg mixture into nut mixture, then, with floured hand, press dough just until blended.

4. Divide dough in half. On prepared cookie sheet, with floured hands, shape each half into 9-inch log, placing logs 3 inches apart. Bake 35 minutes. Cool logs on cookie sheet on wire rack 30 minutes. Transfer logs to cutting board. With serrated knife, cut logs crosswise on the diagonal into ¼-inch-thick slices. Place slices, cut side down, on 2 cookie sheets.

5. Bake biscotti, on 2 oven racks, 15 minutes, rotating cookie sheets between upper and lower racks halfway through baking. Transfer biscotti to wire racks to cool.

6. Store Triple-Nut Biscotti in tightly covered container at room temperature up to 3 weeks or in freezer up to 3 months.

- Avoid fragile, buttery cookies that can disintegrate en route. Opt for heftier varieties like our Chocolate Chip Jumbos (page 25).

- Cushion each cookie. Wrap cookies individually or in pairs (place the flat bottoms together) using foil, plastic wrap, or cellophane bags, then place in self-sealing plastic bags. Package similar cookies together—crisp cookies will get soggy if placed next to soft ones.

- Line a sturdy container, like a small cardboard box, plastic shoe box, or metal tin with Bubble Wrap, foam peanuts, or crumpled waxed or parchment paper. Carefully nestle the cookies inside the container, and seal with tape or tie tightly with ribbon.

- Place the container in a heavyweight cardboard shipping box. Add enough crumpled newspaper, Bubble Wrap, or foam peanuts to prevent shifting. Write *fragile* and *perishable* on all sides of the box.

- Plan ahead. Cookies shipped on a Thursday will sit in a warehouse all weekend, so mail early in the week.

Crunchy, crumbly Italian biscotti make welcome gifts. Our chocolate-filled, triple-nut, and dried-fruit varieties offer delicious options for every name on Santa's list (or yours).

Dried-Fruit Biscotti

From Redbook
Prep 45 minutes
Cook 1 hour
Makes about 4 dozen cookies

- 3 **cups all-purpose flour**
- 1 **Tbsp. baking powder**
- ½ **tsp. salt**
- 3 **large eggs**
- 1 **cup sugar**
- ½ **cup (1 stick) unsalted butter, melted**
- 1 **tsp. almond extract**
- 1 **tsp. vanilla extract**
- ½ **cup almonds, chopped**
- ½ **cup pistachios, chopped**
- ½ **cup dried cranberries**
- ½ **cup each dried apricots, dried papaya, and dried pineapple, diced**
- ¼ **cup crystallized ginger, finely chopped**

1. Preheat oven to 325°F. Grease 2 large cookie sheets. In bowl, whisk flour, baking powder, and salt.

2. In a bowl, with mixer on medium speed, beat eggs and sugar for another minute. Add butter and extracts; beat until blended. With mixer on low speed, gradually add flour mixture, beating just until blended. Stir in nuts, dried fruit, and ginger.

3. Divide dough into 3 equal pieces. On 1 cookie sheet, shape 2 pieces of dough into 12- by 2-inch logs, 3 inches apart. Repeat with the remaining piece of dough on second cookie sheet.

4. Bake 25 to 30 minutes, or until firm, rotating cookie sheets once. Gently loosen logs with a spatula and let cool on cookie sheets. Reduce oven to 275°F. Gently slide logs onto a cutting board. With a serrated knife, cut logs into ½-inch-thick diagonal slices. Place slices on cookie sheets. Bake 25 to 30 minutes, turning once, or until dry. Let cool on wire racks.

All Through the House

There's no place like home for the holidays, especially
when it's decorated with inexpensive,
inspired touches brimming with Christmas spirit

Go
Green!

Spruce It Up

Supermarket seedlings, popped into pails and arrayed along a candlelit mantel, create a wintry woodland scene. Hanging below: a bead garland accessorized with sleek, sculptural ornaments (secured with floral wire).

Perfect Pears

Ripe Bartlett pears serve as edible name-card holders. A pearl-topped pin fastens the placecards to the pears. Pears also appear, accompanied by greenery and tiny ornaments, in a pretty, DIY-on-a-dime centerpiece.

Stick to a pared-down palette for a chic, simple look. Soothing green tones—moss, mint, pine—are a subtle, natural choice.

Door Prize

Bundled together with floral wire, fragrant greenery (yew, holly, spruce, and eucalyptus) makes a grand entrance. Use twine to knot ornaments onto a wooden floral pick; push pick tightly into the boughs. Finish with a bow-tied satin ribbon.

Package Deal

Wrap all the presents under your tree in hues that harmonize with green, and top with mini ornaments. All is calm, all looks right.

Ornament Inspirations

With a little imagination, you can see everyday objects in a festive new light:

1. A vintage Audubon book yielded these images. We turned them into tree-trimmers by color-copying them onto card stock, then cutting out the birds and punching holes at the tops.

2. Scraps of wrapping paper look pretty as a picture when tucked inside nickel frames.

3. The stems of tomato pincushions make for easy hanging.

4. Coated in glossy white spray paint, skeleton keys feel fresh.

5. Vintage mini baking molds add a sweet touch to any tree; simply hot-glue ribbon loops to their backs and hang.

6. Grosgrain ribbons become eye-catching bows.

7. Spray-painted white, pinecones really pop against evergreen boughs.

No need to spend a bundle on trimmings for your tree. You probably already own these treasures, or others like them.

Eco-Smart Trees

Support local agriculture and buy a Christmas tree grown in your area. You can find nearby farms at localharvest.org. Afterward, compost the tree.

The shining star of this bird-themed creation is an egg-filled nest at the top.

All-Natural Noël

Crowned by a twig star and decked with a garland of red burlap, a towering Tannenbaum delights with DIY ornaments: dried orange slices and lady apples, walnuts gilded with gold paint, brown paper cornucopias filled with berries, mini cranberry wreaths, and tucked-in pinecones. Underneath, presents are adorned with equally organic flourishes, such as holly leaves and kumquats.

▲ Clementine and Clove Pomanders

With their thin skins, clementines are ideal for transforming into petite pomanders like these. Pencil various designs onto the fruit, then insert cloves. Heap them in a burlap-lined bowl, and tuck in clippings from your Christmas tree.

◀ Homemade Wrapping Paper

With a little imagination, brown parcel paper, some twine, festive ribbon, and nature-made embellishments are all you need to dress up gifts. Wrap your presents as usual; add the twine or ribbon. Then, use floral wire to attach kumquats, holly sprigs, and other seasonal decor to add a burst of color.

Orange Ornaments ▶

1. Cut oranges crosswise into ¾-inch slices to create a pinwheel effect, trying to keep the slices as uniform as possible in thickness.

2. Lay orange slices on a baking sheet in the oven set at the lowest temperature (around 150°F.). Leave them to bake for about four hours, then turn with a spatula, checking every hour until they seem almost dry; they should have a bit of moisture left so they still have an orange color (they will continue to dry at room temperature).

3. Create a tiny hole in the top of each

slice with a small paring knife, and string twine through each to hang on your tree.

Sweet Lady Apples ▶

When selecting these mini apples, try to choose ones that are 2 inches across or smaller so they're not too bulky (or heavy) to hang from the tree branches. To hang: Take a piece of floral wire long enough to poke about one-third of the way through the apple (or until it feels secure), and leave enough wire to fashion a hook at the top so you can hang the apple on your tree.

▲ Christmas Tree Cornucopia

Add these handmade horns of plenty to your tree as vessels for sprigs of holly and berries.

1. Use a 12- to 14-inch bowl to make circles on brown paper or brown grocery bags.

2. Cut out each circle, then cut it in half. Fold each semicircle into thirds so that the "corners" come in to form a triple-thick flattened cone.

3. Cut through the three layers along the top to create a scalloped edge. Fold over the scallops in the "front" of the cone (this will be the side that faces the room, if the cone is lying flat on a surface, and the overlapping "corners" are underneath).

4. Squeeze in the sides to create a three-dimensional cone shape; staple together in "back" to secure. Thread cone with twine to hang. Fill cone with holly sprigs and berries.

Santa Claus Is Coming to Town

For kids (And kids at heart),
a spectacular array of
delicious bite-size treats

Ho-Ho Home

1. Salute Christmas spirit: Print letters spelling out BELIEVE in mega type to make this banner.

2. Tiny hats and ho ho ho ornaments made with stick-on letters keep the tannenbaum on theme.

3. Peppermints and a photo turn a vase into a sweet stocking holder.

4. The crowning touch: Santa's hat as tree topper.

5. To craft this ornament, all you need are mini belt buckles, black felt, and a glue gun.

6. For graphic punch, mix crisp black and white dots with traditional Yuletide papers.

7. The traditional late-night treat becomes edible decor.

8. Bring some jingle to stockings by looping on sleigh bells.

Red Buckle Balls

4-inch-diameter red ball ornament

Black felt strip, 1 inch by 8 inches

Small gold belt buckles
(from fabric store)

Hot glue

Feed black felt strip through gold buckle so buckle is centered; wrap felt strip around middle of red ornament. Hot-glue ends of felt strip to back of ball so they just meet.

Red Hat Ornaments

Red felt, cut into 5-inch squares

Red yarn

Small silver jingle bell

White fur fabric,
cut into ¾ inch strips

Hot glue

Place an 8-inch-diameter plate over felt square so its curved edge forms a centered arc on the felt. Trace the quarter-circle shape created by edge of plate, and cut along the line. This creates a triangle with a curved edge. Place felt piece flat on a table and hot-glue end of a small loop of yarn near top of triangle, allowing loop to overhang. Run another piece of yarn through loop and tie tightly, leaving a 1½ inch piece of yarn at end. Tie bell onto that piece, then double back the excess yarn and hot-glue it to felt triangle. Once glue has dried, form felt into a cone; secure with hot glue. Finish by gluing fur to bottom of hat, with seam in back.

Believe Banner

7 sheets 8½- by 11-inch
white printer paper

Variety of scrapbook papers,
cut into 5½-inch squares

Spray adhesive or scrapbooking glue

Hole punch

60 inches of ribbon, cut into six
4-inch strips and two
18-inch strips

Print the individual letters in BELIEVE in 430-point Bodoni font on white paper; cut each into a 4½-inch square with letter centered. Adhere each letter onto a 5½-inch square of patterned scrapbook paper. Punch holes in top two corners of each square; join lettered squares with ribbon tied at each corner, leaving about an inch between cards. Tie longer pieces of ribbon to outer corners of first and last letter and allow to hang down on either side. Affix banner to wall.

Stocking Holder

Rectangular glass container
(we used a 3- by 9-inch one)

12-inch piece of ½-inch-wide
red-and-white ribbon

Photo

Red-and-white peppermints

Hot glue

1 square white sticky-back Velcro

Center one end of ribbon on bottom of glass container and hot-glue in place so when ribbon hangs to the front, right side faces out. Pour some candy into container, slip photo into front, and fill up with candy. Place container on mantel and slip ribbon through stocking's hanging loop, from front to back. Bring end of ribbon back up to bottom of container and adhere with sticky-back Velcro.

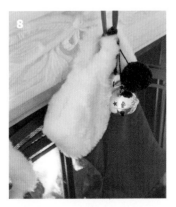

Vintage Tree

Add 1950s-inspired whimsy with a silver tinsel tree. Keep ornaments to one color family, like striking scarlet, for maximum effect.

Cutting-Edge Shapes

You'll never run out of ornaments with this cool, two-dimensional idea:

- Trace geometric or other simple shapes onto colored posterboard or patterned notecards.
- Cut them out, punch holes in them, and hang with ornament hooks.

Tree-Trimming Toolbox

It's inevitable—ornament hooks get lost or broken, or you can't locate the scissors when you most desperately need them. Keep these and all your other tree-trimming essentials handy to ensure the decorating process goes off without a hitch. Stow the supplies in a small toolbox, like the one shown here, and store it with your ornaments for easy access: You'll need:

- wire cutters
- scissors
- ornament hooks
- nylon fishing line
- paper clips
- thin ribbon
- invisible tape
- twine

Go Mod

Use a string of lights to create another "tree" anywhere in your house. Make it big or small—all you need is a wall.

Give tradition an update
with a tree that
reflects recent decades,
or shows off your collection
of flea-market finds.

Find Your Style

Pick up bright antique
ornaments at tag sales,
mix with fanciful feathers and
a multicolored garland, and
top it all with a pretty pink
bow. Now you've got a tree
that's one of a kind.

Welcome guests to your home with a wreath on the front door, above a mantel, in a window—or any place at all.

Berried Treasure

A circle of winterberry branches brightens a mantel scene.

1. Cut 40 to 50 branches of winterberries to measure between 10 and 16 inches long.

2. Using green florist wire, attach the larger branches to a 16- to 18-inch wire frame one at a time, overlapping as you go.

3. Continue adding smaller branches until wreath looks full; use a glue gun when the wiring becomes too difficult.

Recycled "Holly"

Holiday greeting cards are turned into holly leaves for this eco-minded decoration.

1. With a stencil, trace holly-leaf shapes onto old cards and cut out.

2. Using a glue gun, attach a toothpick onto the back of each of the leaves to form a 1-inch pick at the "bottom" of each holly leaf.

3. Take a 10-inch foam wreath and insert these leaf picks around the shape until it is completely covered, fanning and overlapping them as shown.

4. Cut out more holly leaves as needed to cover the wreath with regifted greetings.

Christmas Ball Wreath

A shimmery stunner takes Christmas ornaments off the tree and onto the wall.

1. Buy a straw wreath about 22 inches in diameter from the crafts store.

2. Using a half-yard of white felt cut into 3-inch-wide strips, wrap each piece around the wreath, pinning to secure and overlapping the edges.

3. Take assorted Christmas balls and attach them to the felt with a low-temperature glue gun, using the smallest balls to fill in holes and gaps.

NOTE: This is a great way to use older ornaments that may not look good from all angles. You can also add small stars, snowflakes, or other shapes or trinkets to give your wreath a unique look. Hang with wire, wrapped securely around "top" of wreath. (You'll need to add the wire before you cover the wreath completely with ornaments.)

Sugar-Coated-Fruit Ring

Glitter and organza ribbon turn artificial fruit into a beautiful symbol of the season's abundance.

1. Gather an assortment of artificial fruit (oranges, pears, lemons, apples, etc.). Insert a florist pick into each fruit.

2. Roll them, one at a time, in tacky glue (such as Aleenes, available at crafts stores), then Epsom salts, and finally white, iridescent glitter.

3. Push the picks into a brick of foam and allow the fruit to dry completely.

4. Wrap an 18-inch straw wreath in lime-green ribbon and pin to secure. Use a craft knife to make holes in the ribbon where you will be placing the fruit.

5. Stick the dry fruit into the wreath, starting with the larger pieces. Use a glue gun to secure them.

6. Attach an organza ribbon with wire, then loosely wrap the ribbon ends around the wreath.

Making these simple
Christmas crafts is good fun,
but enjoying them for seasons
to come is even better.

Time for a Kiss

Encourage holiday smooches with this
no-fuss kissing ball.

1. Wrap a four-inch foam ball in a 14-inch
fabric square; secure with a rubber band.

2. Thread the end of 1½ yards of ribbon
down through the band, around the ball,
and up through the band's other side so
ribbon ends match up (knot them to
hang the ball).

3. Wrap 14 inches of ribbon around the
ball's other side (crossing first ribbon, as
shown); tuck ends into band.

4. Hide band with a shimmery bow and
festive sprigs. Hang in doorway.

Merry Mistletoe

The ancient Druids considered
this evergreen a sacred plant,
with mysterious and medicinal
powers. Now we know it's
powerful enough to elicit a kiss!

Horse Play

Hang a gingerbread horse on your tree. Cookies in the shape of Dala horses—ponies that are a Swedish icon—make for the sweetest ornaments. Finish with white icing.

Snow Adorable

Build a Frosty that will last no matter what the forecast.

1. Roll balls of oven-bake clay (find it at the crafts store) into tiered sizes, with the bottom, largest one roughly three inches tall.

2. Wind white yarn (whatever is in your budget: anything from fuzzy white angora to inexpensive acrylic yarn will work) around each ball until clay is completely covered. To connect the snowman, break a wooden skewer down to size, then spear the top and bottom of the "tummy," sticking on the "head" and "bottom" on either side.

3. Give your snowpal evergreen sprigs for arms and a sense of style by dressing him up with assorted buttons, pins, construction paper, and felt, all from the crafts store.

Tune Up Your Tree

Create noteworthy ornaments that show off favorite songs.

1. Copy sheet music; then gather scissors, white glue, ribbon, and cording from a crafts store, and a corrugated cardboard box (break it down and peel apart the layers to reveal ridged sheets).

2. Cut out stars from cardboard and music; tie bows of cording; layer stars and bows as shown; glue. Once dry, glue a ribbon loop to the top back of each ornament to hang.

Warm Wishes

Spell out holiday greetings using simple alphabet stamps and tags from an office-supply store.

Tie It On

Make place settings look like presents with napkin rings crafted from leftover wrapping paper, rickrack, and double-sided tape.

1. Snip strips of paper roughly 1½ inches wide and 5 inches long (test one on your linens, as the size varies depending on your rolled-up napkin's thickness).

2. Wrap the paper around napkins, using double-sided tape to affix.

3. Cut out 6-inch lengths of rickrack, and tie around the bands for a finished look. Set the table and wait for guests to open them.

Snow Days

Here's a simple way to create a striking centerpiece for a hallway table: Rally the kids to join you in making paper snowflakes. Gather scissors and stacks of red and white construction paper, and snip. Hang your best work on branches (spray-painted white), then arrange in a pretty white vase. Or, poke holes in the flakes, tie on string, and suspend in a window.

Get Star-Struck

For luminarias, cut red paper bags in half with decorative scissors, and trim the tops of white or brown bags. Pop out stars with a star-shaped hole punch. Insert taller bags into red bags; half-fill with sand; add LED candles or glass votives.

Raid the Kitchen

Find inspiration in your cabinets:
Tie long lengths of ribbon to cookie
cutters and display them above a
window seat or in a doorway.
Or deck out a charming homespun
Christmas tree if you have more
than a baker's dozen.

Super-Simple
Touches

All the Trimmings

A sweet alternative to store-bought cards, these greetings put your tree-decorating skills to work—on a small scale.

1. Download our illustration at country living.com/dec-templates, and print in color onto 8½- by 11-inch card stock.

2. Fold the stock in half lengthwise, creasing with a bone folder. For the card at top left, attach small bugle beads and paillettes to the tree (use craft glue for all designs). To replicate the middle version, cut out ornaments (made by tracing a button), a tree base, and a star from patterned fabrics and adhere. Make the last card by zigzagging a length of ribbon across the tree.

3. Fold the ends under and glue, then try other widths of ribbon to craft a base, star, and gift. Or use your imagination, and whatever supplies you have on hand, to make your own one-of-a-kind cards.

Festive Footnote

Your staircase can say "Happy Holidays" with a display of Christmas cards or kids' designs: Put double-stick tape at end of a 1- or 2-foot length of ribbon (try grosgrain or satin); attach to stair tread. Affix cards or artwork to the ribbon; tie a bauble on the hanging end if desired.

Make a Tree of Cards

Save your mantel from a paper blizzard and hang cards on your door instead.

1. To craft the card tree, you'll need two wood dowels. Cut them into five segments, starting with eight inches wide and enlarging each piece by two inches.

2. Fold two yards of ribbon in half, then place the shortest dowel about six inches from the fold, spacing the rest about five inches apart from one another.

3. Hot-glue so the dowels are sandwiched between the two ribbon tails. Attach your favorite greetings to the dowels with small binder clips and hang.

Try one of these clever ideas for making your own holiday greeting cards or displaying those you've received from friends.

Holiday History

The first Christmas card was sent in London in 1843. Hallmark published its first cards 72 years later. Christmas is now the largest card-sending holiday in the United States.

Change
of
Hearth

Make your fireplace the most festive spot in the house with these elegant, wallet-friendly transformations.

Come December, as soon as stockings find their way out of storage, the mantel becomes every home's focal point. To take this one (below) from everyday to holiday, we decorated with items most people already have on hand this time of year, such as greeting cards, ribbons, and tissue paper. Finishing touches unearthed from the backyard (free pinecones!) give the scene a rustic feel, while inexpensive crafts-store extras, like mica snow, add subtle sparkle. The result: a winter wonderland with a sophisticated look that belies its modest cost.

> Give your mantel (and fireplace) a makeover for the holidays. It couldn't be easier to do.

Before

Candleholders

Small glass votives filled with pearlescent mica flakes offer an unexpected home for tapers. Provide extra stability with candle putty.

Pinecones

A few light spritzes of fake snow turn these backyard finds into frosty works of art. When they're perched underneath glass cloches misted with the same icy spray, the entire scene resembles an ultra-refined snow globe.

Understated Stockings

Alternatives to traditional red-and-green felt, these rustic booties telegraph a desire for gifts—without going over-the-top. Trim with vintage lace or decorate with seed pods. Stocking at far right is made out of recycled magazines.

Poinsettias

What's not to love about these fuss-free flowers? Fashioned from paper, our fake blossoms, perched atop real twig stems, don't require watering and keep their cheery color all year long.

Red Origami Flower

1. Accordion-fold a 6-inch-square sheet of red foil origami paper in half-inch increments.

2. Cut the paper perpendicular to the folds you made to create 2-inch-wide stacks.

3. Snip a corner off one end of the stack to create a pointed tip.

4. Poke a threaded needle through the bottom of the stack, pull the string tight and knot the end.

5. Fan the petals out, gluing the end pieces together to form a circle.

6. Push a twig through the center for a stem. Repeat for each stack.

White Tissue-Paper Flower

1. Cut out a 3- by 7-inch rectangle from a stack of four pieces of tissue paper.

2. Fold the stack in half; then cut out a petal shape, lining up the base of the petal with the fold (leave the paper connected at the fold).

3. Unfold and rotate the petals so they overlap and form a flower.

4. Bend one end of a 4-inch piece of wire into a tiny loop; pierce the other end down through the center of the flower and thread the flower onto the wire.

5. Scrunch the petals forward and secure to the wire with floral tape; then open them and fluff. Wrap the remaining wire around a twig.

Cards Sharp

A pre-stretched canvas (available at art-supply stores) placed in front of an unlit fireplace serves as the perfect blank slate for displaying holiday greetings. Simply string ribbons across the canvas, staple in back, then hang cards from decorative metal clips.

Mirror

A plain mirror gets a seasonal update with this shimmering frame of tissue paper leaves. We alternated between silver and white and taped the foliage at varying angles to add dimension.

Glass Act

For a simply stunning display,
fill otherwise unused glass
vases and bowls with an array
of ornaments in unexpected
color combos like blue and gold
or red and orange.

More Is More!

Gather together groups of
small objects, display
them in an eye-catching
container, and you've got easy,
instant decorations.

Wicker Wonderland

Turn an old hamper or a large basket into an attractive present wrangler. Wrap it with a bright bow and show off gifts on the big day.

Bowl of Sweets

Transform everyday fruits, above, into glittery holiday decorations. To make, just roll apples and pomegranates in pasteurized egg whites, then in sugar for a frosty, wintry effect.

Let There Be Light

Arrange candles in assorted shapes and sizes on a pretty tray and festoon with berries to brighten up a dark corner or tabletop. Choosing candleholders in warm copper and dark glass enhances the effect.

Go Nuts

Heaped with walnuts, cranberries, and kumquats, a cylinder vase displays festive flavors. Place a tall (8- to 12-inch) pillar candle and holder inside the vase; surround with fruits and nuts.

Bough Wow

Bring enchantment to bare branches with sparkling votives in homespun holders.

1. To make the handle, thread the ends of a 6-inch length of 20-gauge floral wire through two slots in a hose clamp.

2. Attach the clamp to a canning jar, and pop a candle inside. Suspend from limbs that you can easily check on.

Lit from Within

Highlight a window wreath (and help St. Nick and other visitors navigate the night) by lining up festive luminaries below the sill (top left). To get this bright idea in the bag, stencil letters onto green and red paper sacks and cut out with an X-Acto knife. Fill each with a few inches of sand (to keep it from toppling over) and a votive or LED candle. Never leave lighted candles unattended.

Rings of Fire

Artificial trees can't hold a candle to this woodsy Tannenbaum (above). Pack a galvanized tub with sand, and affix a grapevine wreath to its rim. Poke a trio of 4-foot birch poles into the sand. Wire on gradually smaller wreaths; secure candles with wire (and keep a careful eye out), or simply trim with twinkle lights.

Jingle Balls

Even a birdbath can get into the spirit of the season. For this flight of fancy (left), fill a small bucket with snow or sand, center inside the bowl's base, and top with evergreen sprigs and battery-powered orbs. The finishing touch: pinecones.

Christmas Dinners

For a memory-making holiday meal, start with
a succulent bird or roast, then add some new twists on the stuffing,
potatoes, and sides you love. Here's inspiration.

Turkey Two Ways

You can prepare this golden bird with wild mushroom gravy or roasted-garlic gravy.

Shop Smart

Include at least two cans of chicken broth on your holiday grocery list so you'll have enough to add to the gravies in step 9.

Roast Turkey with Wild Mushroom Gravy

From Good Housekeeping
Prep 55 minutes **Cook** 3¾ hours **Makes** 14 main-dish servings

NOTE: You can choose the alternative gravy option at the end of the recipe.

- 1 **fresh or frozen (thawed) turkey (14 lbs.)**
- 1 **lemon**
- 1 **cup loosely packed fresh parsley leaves, chopped**
- ¼ **cup loosely packed fresh sage leaves, chopped**
- 2 **Tbsp. fresh thyme leaves, chopped**
  Salt and pepper
- 1 **Tbsp. olive oil**
- 1 **medium carrot, coarsely chopped**
- 1 **medium celery stalk, coarsely chopped**

- 2 **small onions, each cut into quarters**
- 2 **Tbsp. margarine or butter**
- 8 **oz. sliced white mushrooms**
- 6 **oz. sliced cremini mushrooms**
- 4 **oz. sliced shiitake mushrooms**
- 2–3 **cans (14 to 14.5 oz. each) chicken broth**
- ⅓ **cup all-purpose flour**
  Fresh herbs and fruit for garnish

1. Preheat oven to 325°F. Remove giblets and neck from turkey cavity; set aside. Discard liver or save for another use. Cut neck into several large pieces. Rinse turkey inside and out with cold running water and drain well; pat dry with paper towels. Place turkey, breast side up, on small rack in large roasting pan (17- by 11½-inch). Scatter giblets and neck in pan around turkey.

2. Grate 1 tsp. lemon peel and place in small bowl. Cut lemon in half and set aside. To grated lemon peel, add parsley, sage, thyme, 2 tsp. salt, and 1 tsp. freshly ground black pepper, and stir until blended.

3. In medium bowl, place olive oil, carrot, and celery; stir in 2 Tbsp. herb mixture to coat vegetables. Place vegetable mixture in pan around turkey. Sprinkle remaining herb mixture inside body and neck cavities, and rub all over outside of turkey. Squeeze juice from lemon halves into both cavities, and place lemon halves and 4 onion quarters in body cavity. Place remaining 4 onion quarters in pan around turkey. Fold wings under back of turkey. If drumsticks are not held by band of skin or stuffing clamp, tie legs together with string.

4. Cover turkey with a loose tent of foil; roast 2½ hours. Remove foil and roast 1¼ hours longer.

5. About 20 minutes before turkey finishes roasting, cook mushrooms for gravy: In 12-inch nonstick skillet on medium, heat margarine until melted. Add all mushrooms and cook, covered, 6 minutes. Uncover and cook 11 to 12 minutes longer or until tender and golden, stirring occasionally. Remove skillet from heat and set aside.

6. Turkey is done when temperature on meat thermometer, inserted into thickest part of thigh next to body, reaches 175° to 180°F. and breast temperature reaches 165°F.

7. When turkey is done, carefully lift from roasting pan and tilt to allow juices to run into pan. Place turkey on platter; cover loosely with foil.

8. Complete the gravy: Remove rack from roasting pan. Strain pan drippings into 4-cup liquid measuring cup or medium bowl, leaving giblets and neck in pan. Let drippings stand for about 1 minute to allow fat to separate from meat juices. Spoon ¼ cup fat from drippings into 2-quart saucepan. Discard any fat remaining in pan.

COMPANY'S COMING

How Much Do I Need?

Cooking for a crowd can be complicated—you know how much stuffing to make for eight people, but how much for 20? Solution: our at-a-glance guidelines for 11 holiday basics, showing the minimum amount you'll need to buy whether you're entertaining eight or 24 or various numbers in between.

DISH	8 SERVINGS	10 SERVINGS	12 SERVINGS	16 SERVINGS	20 SERVINGS	24 SERVINGS
Turkey	8 lbs.	10 lbs.	12 lbs.	16 lbs.	20 lbs.	24 lbs.
Stuffing (dry mix)	8 oz.	10 oz.	12 oz.	16 oz.	20 oz.	24 oz.
White potatoes	3 lbs. (6 lg.)	3½ lbs. (7 lg.)	4½ lbs. (9 lg.)	6 lbs. (12 lg.)	7½ lbs. (15 lg.)	9 lbs. (18 lg.)
Butternut squash	3½ lbs. (2 sm.)	4 lbs. (2 med.)	5 lbs. (2 lg.)	6¾ lbs. (3 med.)	8 lbs. (4 med.)	10 lbs. (4 lg.)
Brussels sprouts	2 (10-oz.) containers	3 (10-oz.) containers	3 (10-oz.) containers	4 (10-oz.) containers	5 (10-oz.) containers	6 (10-oz.) containers
Green beans	2 lbs.	2½ lbs.	3 lbs.	4 lbs.	5 lbs.	6 lbs.
Sweet potatoes	3 lbs. (3 lg.)	3¾ lbs. (4 lg.)	4½ lbs. (5 lg.)	6 lbs. (6 lg.)	7½ lbs. (8 lg.)	9 lbs. (9 lg.)
Pearl onions	2 (10-oz.) containers	2 (10-oz.) containers	3 (10-oz.) containers	3 (10-oz.) containers	4 (10-oz.) containers	4 (10-oz.) containers
Cranberry sauce (canned)	2 (16-oz.) cans	2 (16-oz.) cans	3 (16-oz.) cans	3 (16-oz.) cans	4 (16-oz.) cans	4 (16-oz.) cans
Creamed spinach (frozen)	3 (10-oz.) pkgs.	4 (10-oz.) pkgs.	4 (10-oz.) pkgs.	6 (10-oz.) pkgs.	8 (10-oz.) pkgs.	8 (10-oz.) pkgs.
Pie	1 or 2 (9-inch) pies	2 (9-inch) pies	2 (9-inch) pies	2 or 3 (9-inch) pies	3 (9-inch) pies	3 or 4 (9-inch) pies

9. Place roasting pan over 2 burners on top of range, and cook 2 to 4 minutes on medium-high to brown giblets, neck, and bits on bottom of pan, stirring constantly. Carefully add 1 cup chicken broth to roasting pan and boil about 3 minutes or until broth is reduced by half, stirring until browned bits are loosened from bottom of pan. Strain broth mixture into meat juices in measuring cup; add any additional meat juices on platter. Discard giblets and neck. Add enough additional broth to meat-juice mixture in cups to equal 4 cups total. (Save any leftover broth for another use.)

10. With wire whisk, mix flour into fat in saucepan; cook on medium 3 to 4 minutes or until mixture turns golden-brown, whisking constantly. While still whisking, gradually add meat-juice mixture to saucepan; cook on medium-high until mixture boils and thickens, stirring frequently; boil 1 minute. Stir in mushroom mixture; heat through. Pour gravy into gravy boat and serve with turkey. Garnish platter with herbs and fruit. Makes about 6 cups gravy.

ROAST TURKEY WITH ROASTED-GARLIC GRAVY: Prepare turkey and gravy as above, but omit margarine, mushrooms, and all of step 5. In step 3, separate 1 head garlic into cloves; do not peel. Add garlic to bowl with vegetable mixture. In step 8, before straining pan drippings, with spatula or back of spoon, press garlic cloves, still in roasting pan, to squeeze soft roasted garlic into pan drippings; discard peels. Complete recipe as in steps 9 and 10. Makes about 4 cups gravy.

Remember, It's Just A Turkey

Whether you're a first-timer or a seasoned cook, our tips will help you confidently prep and roast the bird.

WHAT TO BUY

• Frozen turkeys are widely available and often on sale during the holidays. Some are pre-basted to enhance juiciness. You can buy them well in advance of preparation, but you'll need to allow enough time for them to thaw.

• Fresh turkeys are preferred by many people but are usually more expensive, have a shorter shelf life, and may need to be special-ordered. Don't buy one more than two days ahead.

HOW MUCH TO BUY

• Estimate 1 pound uncooked turkey per person to ensure enough meat for a festive dinner—and leftovers.

HOW TO THAW

• The best way: Place frozen turkey (still in packaging) in a pan on the bottom shelf of the refrigerator. Allow 24 hours thawing time for every 4 to 5 pounds. A thawed bird can keep up to 4 days in the fridge. Last-minute solution: Submerge a still-wrapped turkey in cold water. Allow 30 minutes of thawing time per pound; change water every 30 minutes. Cook turkey immediately.

HOW TO ROAST

• Place the turkey (breast side up) on a rack in a large roasting pan in an oven preheated to 325°F. If you don't have a rack, place 2 or 3 large carrots crosswise underneath the bird to ensure good heat circulation.

• For moist meat, cover with foil from the start—but remove it during the last hour of roasting to produce browner, crispier skin.

• Roast turkey 3 to 3¾ hours for a 12- to 14-pounder (that's approximately 15 to 17 minutes per pound for an unstuffed bird).

• Use an instant-read meat thermometer to test doneness. Turkey should be taken out of the oven when the thickest part of the thigh (next to but not touching the bone) reaches 175°F. and the breast reaches 165°F.

• If the turkey is fully cooked earlier than expected, wrap the entire bird and pan with foil and place a large bath towel on top to keep it hot and moist for 1 hour. For safety reasons, never leave turkey standing at room temperature any longer than 2 hours.

Turkey Breast with Spinach-Herb Stuffing

From Good Housekeeping
Prep 30 minutes
Cook 2¼ hours
Makes 10 main-dish servings

- 1 **Tbsp. olive oil**
- 1 **small onion, finely chopped**
- 2 **medium celery stalks, finely chopped**
- 1 **package (10 oz.) frozen chopped spinach, thawed and squeezed dry**
- ½ **tsp. dried thyme**
- ¼ **tsp. dried sage**
- 2¾ **cups chicken broth**
  Salt and pepper
- ½ **loaf sliced firm white bread (8 oz.), lightly toasted and cut into ½-inch cubes**
- 1 **bone-in turkey breast (7 lbs.)**
- 4 **tsp. cornstarch**

1. Preheat oven to 350°F.

2. Prepare stuffing: In 12-inch nonstick skillet on medium, in oil, cook onion and celery 10 to 12 minutes or until vegetables are lightly browned and tender, stirring occasionally. Remove skillet from heat; stir in squeezed spinach, thyme, sage, ¾ cup chicken broth, ½ tsp. salt, and ¼ tsp. coarsely ground black pepper. Place bread cubes in large bowl; add spinach mixture and toss to mix well.

3. Pat turkey breast dry with paper towels. With fingertips, gently separate skin from meat on breast, being careful not to break skin. Spread stuffing mixture on meat under skin. Place turkey, skin side up, on rack in small roasting pan (13- by 9-inch). Cover turkey with loose tent of foil.

4. Roast turkey 1 hour and 45 minutes. Remove foil and roast turkey 30 to 40 minutes longer.

5. Transfer turkey to warm platter. Let stand 15 minutes to set juices for easier carving. Make gravy, opposite page.

Make a Great Gravy Remove rack from roasting pan. Pour **drippings** through sieve into 1-cup liquid measuring cup or small bowl. Let drippings stand 1 minute to allow fat to separate from meat juices. Skim and discard fat. Place roasting pan on medium-high, and cook 1 to 2 minutes to brown bits on bottom of pan, stirring. Carefully add ½ **cup chicken broth** and cook 1 minute. Stir **cornstarch** into remaining 1½ cups **broth**, and add with meat juices to roasting pan. Heat to boiling; boil 1 to 2 minutes or until gravy thickens, stirring to loosen brown bits from bottom of pan. Pour gravy (or strain, if you like) into gravy boat; serve with sliced turkey. Makes about 2 cups gravy.

Extra
Easy
Entrée!

Roast Pork Loin with Apples, Potatoes & Sage

From Good Housekeeping
Prep 15 minutes
Cook 50 minutes
Makes 8 main-dish servings

- 3 Tbsp. margarine or butter, softened
- 2 Tbsp. chopped fresh sage leaves
  Salt and pepper
- 1 boneless pork loin roast (about 3 lbs.), trimmed of fat
- 1½ lbs. baby red potatoes, each cut in half
- 1 large onion, chopped
- 1½ lbs. Gala or Jonagold apples (3 to 4 medium), cored and cut into 8 wedges

1. Preheat oven to 450°F. In small bowl, combine 1 Tbsp. margarine, 1 Tbsp. chopped sage, ½ tsp. salt, and ¼ tsp. coarsely ground pepper. With hands, rub sage mixture all over pork loin.

2. In 15½- by 10½-inch jelly-roll pan, melt remaining 2 Tbsp. margarine in oven. Remove pan from oven. Add potatoes, onion, ½ tsp. salt, and remaining 1 Tbsp. chopped sage; toss to coat. Push potatoes and onion to edges of pan, and set small roasting rack in center; place pork on rack. Roast 20 minutes.

3. Add apples to pan, around pork, and roast 30 to 40 minutes longer, depending on thickness of pork, or until meat thermometer inserted into center of pork reaches 145°F. (Internal temperature of pork will rise 5° to 10°F. upon standing.)

4. Transfer pork to warm platter; let stand 15 minutes to set juice for easier slicing. With slotted spoon, transfer potatoes, onion, and apples to platter. Pour pan drippings into cup. Skim off and discard fat from drippings. Serve pork, sliced, with drippings.

Ham Takes the Stage

Yes, ham can be the centerpiece of a healthy meal—just choose a piece that's lean, low-sodium, and smoked (to reduce the fat).

Glazed Ham with Apricots From Good Housekeeping

Prep 35 minutes **Cook** 2¼ hours **Makes** 16 main-dish servings

- 1 fully cooked bone-in smoked half ham (7 lbs.)
- 1 package (6 oz.) dried apricot halves
- 2 Tbsp. whole cloves
- ½ cup orange marmalade or apricot jam
- 2 Tbsp. country-style Dijon mustard with seeds

1. Preheat oven to 325°F. Remove skin and trim all but ⅛ inch fat from ham. Secure apricots with cloves to fat side of ham in rows, leaving space between apricots. Place ham, fat side up, on rack in roasting pan (17- by 11½-inch); add 1 cup water. Cover pan tightly with foil.

2. Bake 2 hours. After ham has baked 1 hour and 45 minutes, prepare glaze: In 1-quart saucepan, heat marmalade and mustard to boiling on medium-high heat. Remove foil from ham and carefully brush with some of the glaze. Continue to bake the ham 30 to 40 minutes longer or until meat thermometer reaches 135°F., brushing with glaze every 15 minutes. The internal temperature of the ham will rise 5° to 10°F. upon standing. (Don't worry if some of the apricots may fall off into the pan as you glaze.)

3. Transfer ham to cutting board; cover and let stand 20 minutes to ensure easier slicing. Slice ham and serve with apricots from pan.

Beef Tenderloin with Shallot Sauce

From Good Housekeeping **Prep** 45 minutes **Cook** 50 minutes **Makes** 12 main-dish servings

- 3 **large shallots, finely chopped (1¼ cups)**
- 4 **Tbsp. fresh tarragon leaves, chopped, plus more for garnish**
- 2 **Tbsp. olive oil**
  Salt and pepper
- 1 **whole beef tenderloin (5 lbs.), trimmed and tied**
- 2 **Tbsp. white wine vinegar**
- 1 **cup beef broth**
- 2 **Tbsp. margarine or butter**
  Rosemary sprigs and bay leaves for garnish

1. Preheat oven to 425°F. In small bowl, combine half of shallots, 2 Tbsp. chopped tarragon, 1 Tbsp. oil, 1½ tsp. salt, and 2 tsp. coarsely ground black pepper. Rub mixture all over tenderloin. Place tenderloin (see "BYOB" below, for trimming instructions), smooth side up, on rack in large roasting pan (17- by 13½-inch). Roast tenderloin 45 to 50 minutes or until thermometer inserted in center reaches 135°F. Internal temperature of meat will rise 5° to 10°F. (medium-rare) upon standing. Or, roast to desired doneness.

2. Transfer to platter; tent loosely with aluminum foil. Let stand 10 to 15 minutes for easier slicing.

3. Meanwhile, prepare sauce: Place roasting pan over 2 burners on top of range on medium, and add remaining 1 Tbsp. oil and remaining shallots. Cook 1 to 2 minutes or until tender, stirring. Add vinegar and cook 1 to 2 minutes or until reduced by half, stirring and scraping pan to loosen any browned bits. Add beef broth, bring to a simmer, and cook 4 to 5 minutes or until reduced by half, stirring and scraping pan. Remove from heat; stir in margarine until melted. Carefully pour sauce through fine-mesh strainer into gravy boat. Stir in remaining 2 Tbsp. tarragon and any accumulated beef juices on platter. Makes about ¾ cup sauce.

4. Remove twine from tenderloin and discard. Garnish platter with rosemary sprigs and bay leaves; sprinkle tenderloin with additional chopped tarragon. To serve, cut tenderloin into slices and serve with sauce.

BYOB
(Be Your Own Butcher)

When we asked our market's meat department for a beef tenderloin, they offered us a beautiful 5-pound roast— for $120! No way, not even for Christmas dinner. So we clarified: We wanted a whole, untrimmed tenderloin. The butcher brought out a 6½-pound slab sealed in its wholesale packaging. It wasn't pretty— but it was $35. The savings far outweigh the work of trimming it yourself. Follow our simple method below.

REMOVE THE CHAIN

On one side of the tenderloin, the ragged, narrow chain muscle runs the length of the meat. (A shorter, smoother, rounder muscle is attached to the other side; leave that in place.) Gently pull the chain away from the loin, and with a sharp boning knife, use short strokes to cut off the muscle, starting at the narrow end. Reserve the chain for later use.

CUT OUT THE FAT

Slice away the two large fat deposits between the shorter, intact muscle and the loin, without detaching the muscle. With your fingers, pick off any bits of remaining fat from the roast's surface. Discard all fat.

SLICE OFF THE SILVER SKIN

A thin, pearlescent membrane of connective tissue covers one side of a tenderloin. To remove, slide your boning knife just under the silver skin, one inch from its narrow end, creating a 1-inch-wide cut. Using a slow sawing motion, with the knife angled toward the top of the loin, separate the end of the silver skin from the meat. Hold the freed piece taut, turn the knife around, and repeat to cut off the remaining silver skin. Repeat until all of the silver skin is removed from the meat; discard it.

TUCK AND TIE

Fold the 2-inch tapered end under the loin. Using kitchen twine, tie the roast firmly, but not too tightly, at 1½-inch intervals.

Save Time and Money

Cut costs by trimming the meat yourself (see "BYOB," opposite page). Reduce prep time on the big day by rubbing the tarragon-shallot mixture on the trimmed meat up to a day ahead. Then wrap well and refrigerate.

Golden Mashed Potatoes with Fried Onions & Bacon

From Redbook **Prep** 20 minutes **Cook** 30 minutes **Makes** 10 side-dish servings

- 3½ **lbs. large Yukon Gold potatoes, peeled, quartered**
- ½ **lb. carrots, peeled, coarsely shredded**
- 6 **slices smoked bacon**
- 1 **Tbsp. canola oil**
- 1 **large sweet onion, diced**
- 2 **tsp. fresh thyme leaves**
- ½ **cup buttermilk, at room temperature**
- 2 **Tbsp. unsalted butter, softened**
- 2½ **tsp. kosher salt**

1. In a large saucepan, cover potatoes and carrots with 2 inches of cold water, and bring to a boil over high heat. Reduce heat and simmer until vegetables are tender, about 20 minutes.

2. Meanwhile, cook bacon in a large skillet over medium heat until crisp; drain on paper towels. Discard all but 2 Tbsp. of the bacon drippings from skillet; add oil and onion to drippings, and sauté 10 minutes or until softened and lightly brown. Stir in thyme; cook 2 minutes longer.

3. When potatoes are fork-tender, drain in a colander and transfer mixture to a large bowl. Add buttermilk, butter, and salt; mash with a potato masher until potatoes are smooth, with small flecks of carrot visible. Stir in onions. Crumble bacon over top.

Accordion Potatoes

From Good Housekeeping
Prep 10 minutes
Cook 37 minutes
Makes 8 side-dish servings

- 8 large red potatoes (8 oz. each)
- 2 Tbsp. extra virgin olive oil
  Salt and pepper
- 1 Tbsp. chopped fresh parsley leaves
- 1 tsp. chopped fresh thyme leaves

1. Preheat oven to 450°F.
2. Carefully slice each potato thinly without cutting all the way through. Place potatoes on microwave-safe dish and cover with waxed paper. Cook in microwave on High 12 to 15 minutes or until easily pierced with tip of knife.
3. Transfer potatoes to metal baking pan. Carefully drizzle oil between slices. Sprinkle with ½ tsp. salt and ¼ tsp. coarsely ground black pepper. Roast in oven 25 minutes or until lightly browned. Transfer potatoes to platter; sprinkle with herbs.

Knife Tip

An easy trick to ensure that potatoes are sliced as far down as possible without cutting through to the other side is to rest potatoes, one at a time, in the bowl of a wooden spoon or place chopsticks along both long sides of each potato and slice down until the knife can't go any farther.

Twice-Baked Celery-Root Potatoes

From Good Housekeeping **Prep** 30 minutes
Cook 1 hour 10 minutes **Makes** 12 side-dish servings

- 16 medium russet (baking) potatoes (8 oz. each)
- 1 lb. celery root, peeled and cut into 1-inch chunks
- ½ cup milk
- 4 Tbsp. margarine or butter
  Salt and pepper
- ½ cup freshly grated Parmesan cheese
  Chopped parsley for garnish

1. Preheat oven to 450°F.
2. Place potatoes in oven, directly on rack, and bake 45 to 50 minutes or until tender when pierced with knife. Remove from oven and set aside until cool enough to handle. Reset oven temperature to 400°F. Meanwhile, in 3-quart saucepan, place celery root and enough water to cover; heat to boiling on high. Reduce heat to low; cover and simmer 15 minutes or until celery root is tender. Drain.
3. In food processor with knife blade attached, blend celery root with milk, margarine, ¾ tsp. salt, and ¼ tsp. pepper until pureed. Transfer to bowl.
4. When potatoes are cool enough to handle, cut ¼-inch slice from both of the narrow ends of each one, then cut each potato crosswise in half. Stand potato on narrow ends. With spoon, scoop potato from skins into bowl with celery root puree, leaving about ¼ inch of potato with skin. Be careful not to break through bottom of potato. Reserve potato-skin cups. With potato masher, mash potatoes with celery root until almost smooth. Stir in Parmesan.
5. Spray 15½- by 10½-inch jelly-roll pan with nonstick cooking spray. Spoon potato mixture into potato-skin cups, mounding slightly. Place cups in prepared pan. Bake 25 minutes or until heated and lightly browned. (If not baking right away, cover and refrigerate filled potatoes overnight; bake 35 to 40 minutes.) Transfer to platter and sprinkle with parsley to serve.

Make It Ahead

Prepare and bake recipe through step 4; refrigerate up to two days. When ready to complete, bake, uncovered, as in step 5, on bottom rack of oven, increasing final baking time to 55 minutes.

Potato & Root Vegetable Gratin

From Good Housekeeping
Prep 5 minutes
Cook 1¼ hours
Makes 16 side-dish servings

- ¾ cup chicken broth
- 2 Tbsp. margarine or butter
- 1½ lbs. russet (baking) potatoes (3 medium), peeled and thinly sliced
- 1½ lbs. sweet potatoes (3 small), peeled and thinly sliced
- 1 lb. celery root (1 large or 2 small), trimmed, peeled, quartered, and thinly sliced
- 1 lb. parsnips (6 medium), peeled and thinly sliced
  Salt and pepper
- 1 cup heavy or whipping cream
- 2 Tbsp. snipped fresh chives

1. Preheat oven to 400 degrees. In shallow 3½- to 4-quart baking pan, combine broth and margarine; place pan in oven, while oven is preheating, to melt margarine, about 5 minutes.

2. Meanwhile, in large bowl, toss potatoes, celery root, and parsnips with 1¼ tsp. salt and ½ tsp. freshly ground black pepper until well mixed.

3. Remove baking pan from oven. Add broth mixture to vegetables and stir to coat. Spoon vegetable mixture into same baking pan; cover with foil and bake vegetables 40 minutes.

4. Remove pan from oven. In 1-cup liquid measuring cup, heat cream in microwave on High 45 seconds to warm. Pour cream evenly over vegetables in pan.

5. Return baking pan to oven and bake vegetables, uncovered, 30 to 35 minutes longer or until top is golden and vegetables are fork-tender. Let stand 10 minutes before serving. Sprinkle with chives to serve.

Sweet Potato & Zucchini Latkes

From Good Housekeeping **Prep** 15 minutes **Cook** 15 minutes
Makes about 2 dozen (2-inch) latkes

- 1 large egg
- 1 large egg white
- 1 medium zucchini (about 8 oz.)
- 1 medium sweet potato (about 12 oz.), peeled
- ¼ cup finely chopped onion
  Salt and coarsely ground black pepper
- 3 Tbsp. canola oil
  Unsweetened applesauce (optional)

1. Preheat oven to 250°F. In medium bowl, lightly beat egg and egg white; set aside. Cut zucchini lengthwise in half and remove seeds. Coarsely grate zucchini and sweet potato; transfer to bowl with egg. Stir in onion, ¼ tsp. salt, and ⅛ tsp. pepper until combined.

2. In nonstick 12-inch skillet on medium, heat 1 Tbsp. oil until hot. Add zucchini mixture by heaping tablespoons to skillet, gently flattening each with back of spoon. Cook 2 minutes or until edges are golden; flip and cook 2 to 3 minutes longer or until bottoms are golden. Drain on paper towels. Keep latkes warm in oven.

3. Repeat with remaining 2 Tbsp. oil and remaining zucchini mixture. Serve latkes hot with applesauce on side, if you like.

Crispy Pancakes

Prepare the batter right before cooking to prevent excess liquid and soggy cakes; pour off any extra liquid while cooking if necessary.

Wild Rice Pilaf with Pistachios & Cranberries

From Good Housekeeping
Prep 15 minutes
Cook about 70 minutes
Makes 16 side-dish servings

  2 **cups wild rice (12 oz.)**
  6 **cups water**
1½ **cups dried cranberries**
  2 **Tbsp. margarine or butter**
  4 **medium carrots, chopped**
  2 **large celery stalks, chopped**
  1 **large onion (about 12 oz.), chopped**
  2 **cups regular long-grain white rice**
  1 **can (14 to 14½ oz.) chicken broth (1¾ cup)**
     Salt and pepper
 ½ **cup loosely packed fresh parsley leaves, chopped**
  4 **oz. shelled pistachio nuts (½ cup), toasted and chopped**

1. In 4-quart saucepan on high, heat wild rice and 4 cups water to boiling. Reduce heat to low, cover, and simmer 35 to 40 minutes or until wild rice is tender. Stir in cranberries; cook 1 minute. Drain wild rice mixture, if necessary; keep warm in covered saucepan until ready to use.

2. In heavy 5-quart Dutch oven on medium, melt margarine. Add carrots, celery, and onion; cook 13 to 15 minutes or until vegetables are lightly browned. Transfer vegetables to medium bowl, and set aside at room temperature until all rice is done.

3. In same Dutch oven on high, heat white rice, chicken broth, and remaining 2 cups water to boiling. Reduce heat to low; cover pot and simmer 16 to 18 minutes or until all liquid is absorbed.

4. Into white rice, stir wild-rice mixture, vegetable mixture, 1 tsp. salt, and ½ tsp. freshly ground black pepper; cook on medium-low until pilaf is heated through. Gently stir chopped parsley and pistachio nuts into pilaf.

Praline Candied Garnet Yams From Redbook

Prep 22 minutes **Cook** 1 hour 40 minutes **Makes** 10 side-dish servings

  5 **lbs. garnet yams or sweet potatoes, of equal size**
 ½ **cup (1 stick) cold unsalted butter, cut into 8 pieces**
 ½ **cup cane syrup**
  1 **tsp. kosher salt**
 ¼ **tsp. freshly ground black pepper**
 ¾ **cup pecans, coarsely chopped**
 ⅓ **cup each all-purpose flour and packed light-brown sugar**
 ½ **tsp. ground cinnamon**

1. Heat oven to 400°F. Place yams on a baking sheet and roast 50 minutes or until they are just barely tender yet still hold their shape. Let cool completely at room temperature. (This step can be done up to 2 days ahead.)

2. Remove skins and cut yams into ½-inch-thick slices. Butter a 2-quart baking dish with 1 Tbsp. of the butter. Arrange yam slices in dish, slightly overlapping. Heat oven to 375°F.

3. In a small saucepan on medium, combine syrup, salt, pepper, and another 4 Tbsp. of the butter until butter melts; whisk to combine. Pour mixture over yams.

4. In a small bowl, combine pecans, flour, sugar, and cinnamon; add remaining 3 Tbsp. butter and rub in with fingers until mixture is evenly moistened and forms clumps; sprinkle mixture over yams. Bake yams 35 minutes or until topping is browned.

Serves
16!

Go Wild

Wild rice isn't actually rice at all.
It's a grain—the seeds of a grass that
grows in the cold waters of Minnesota
and Canada. Highly nutritious, it has
a distinctive, nutty flavor.

Should You Stuff It?

The best way to prepare stuffing is to bake it in a shallow casserole next to the turkey. If you do stuff the bird, be sure the turkey is fully thawed, and roast it about 30 minutes longer than you would an unstuffed one.

Butternut Squash Stuffing

From Good Housekeeping
Prep 50 minutes
Cook 45 minutes
Makes 16 side-dish servings

- 12 **cups (½-inch cubes) sour-dough bread (from 1-lb. loaf)**
- 8 **oz. bacon, cut crosswise into ½-inch pieces**
- 1 **butternut squash (about 2 lbs.), peeled, seeded, and cut into ½-inch chunks**
- 3 **celery stalks, chopped**
- 8 **oz. shallots (about 4 large), finely chopped (about 1½ cups)**
- 2 **Tbsp. chopped fresh sage leaves**
   Salt
   Black pepper
- 3 **cups chicken broth**

1. Preheat oven to 325°F. Divide bread between 2 large cookie sheets. Place pans on 2 oven racks and toast bread 30 to 35 minutes or until golden, stirring bread and rotating pans between racks halfway through toasting. Let bread cool in pans.

2. Meanwhile, in nonstick 12-inch skillet on medium heat, cook bacon 15 to 20 minutes or until browned, stirring occasionally. With slotted spoon, transfer bacon to large bowl.

3. Remove all but 3 Tbsp. bacon fat from skillet. Add butternut squash, celery, and shallots, and cook on medium-high 15 minutes or until vegetables are tender and shallots are lightly browned. Remove from heat; stir in sage, ¼ tsp. salt, and ¼ tsp. fresh ground black pepper.

4. To bowl with bacon, add bread and broth; mix well. Add vegetable mixture and toss. Use squash mixture to stuff 12- to 16-lbs. turkey, or spoon into greased 13- by 9-inch glass baking dish. Cover baking dish with foil and bake stuffing in preheated 325°F. oven 20 minutes. Remove foil and stir stuffing. Bake 25 minutes longer until lightly browned.

Savory Pear Stuffing
From Good Housekeeping
Prep 10 minutes **Cook** 30 minutes **Makes** 10 side-dish servings

- 1 **Tbsp. olive oil**
- 2 **celery stalks, chopped**
- 2 **large ripe Bartlett pears**
- ½ **cup loosely packed fresh parsley leaves**
- 4 **green onions**
- 3 **cups water**
- 2 **packages (6 oz. each) corn bread stuffing mix**

1. Preheat oven to 425°F.

2. In 4-quart saucepan, heat oil on medium-high until hot. Add chopped celery and cook about 5 minutes, stirring occasionally.

3. Meanwhile, cut pears (with skin on) into ½-inch chunks, chop parsley, and slice green onions.

4. Add water to celery in saucepot; cover and heat to boiling on high. Remove from heat; stir in stuffing mix, pears, parsley, and green onions.

5. Spoon stuffing into shallow 3- to 3½-quart casserole; cover with foil. Bake 20 minutes; uncover and bake 10 minutes longer until top is crusty and stuffing is heated through.

Mushroom Stuffing

From Good Housekeeping **Prep** 40 minutes **Bake** 65 minutes **Makes** 10 side-dish servings

- **1 lb. artisanal whole-grain bread**
- **4 slices bacon**
- **1 medium onion, chopped**
- **4 celery stalks, chopped**
- **1 tsp. poultry seasoning**
- **2 packages (8 oz. each) sliced mushrooms**
- **½ cup loosely packed fresh parsley leaves, chopped**
  Salt and pepper
- **1¾ to 2½ cups chicken broth**

1. Preheat oven to 325°F. Cut bread into ¾-inch cubes (you should have about 8 cups) and place in 15½- by 10½-inch jellyroll pan or large cookie sheet. Toast bread in oven 25 to 30 minutes or until golden and dry, stirring bread halfway through toasting. Cool bread in pan on wire rack.

2. Meanwhile, cut bacon into ½-inch pieces. In 12-inch skillet on medium, cook bacon 8 to 10 minutes or until browned, stirring occasionally. With slotted spoon, transfer bacon to very large bowl.

3. To bacon drippings in skillet, add onion, celery, and poultry seasoning, and cook on medium-high 10 minutes, stirring occasionally. Add mushrooms and cook 10 minutes longer or until vegetables are tender and lightly browned, stirring occasionally.

4. To bowl with bacon, add bread, vegetable mixture, parsley, ¼ tsp. salt, and ¼ tsp. ground black pepper. Gradually drizzle in chicken broth until cubes are moistened.

5. Use stuffing to fill cavity of 12- to 16-lbs. turkey, or spoon into greased 2½- to 3-quart glass or ceramic baking dish. Cover dish with foil and bake stuffing in preheated 325°F. oven 20 minutes. Remove foil and bake 20 to 25 minutes longer or until heated through and lightly browned on top.

Make It Juicy

Artisanal, or hand-shaped, breads vary greatly, so depending on the density of the bread, you may need more or less broth when preparing the stuffing.

A New Take on Sauce

Corn Pudding

From Good Housekeeping
Prep 15 minutes
Bake 45 minutes
Makes 12 side-dish servings

1 **can (14.75 oz.) cream-style corn**
3 **cups fresh corn kernels (from about 6 ears) or 1 bag (16 oz.) frozen corn**
1 **container (16 oz.) sour cream**
¾ **cup cornmeal**
3 **large eggs, separated**
   Salt and coarsely ground black pepper

1. Preheat oven to 350°F. Grease 13-by-9-inch glass or ceramic baking dish; set aside.

2. In large bowl, combine cream-style corn, fresh or frozen corn kernels, sour cream, cornmeal, egg yolks, ½ tsp. salt, and ½ tsp. pepper.

3. In small bowl, with mixer on high speed, beat egg whites until stiff peaks form. Fold whites into corn mixture; pour into prepared baking dish.

4. Bake pudding 45 minutes or until edges are set and center jiggles slightly. Let pudding stand on wire rack 10 minutes to set before serving.

Cranberry-Ginger Chutney

From Good Housekeeping **Prep** 15 minutes
Cook 35 minutes **Makes** 3¾ cups

1 **bag (12 oz.) cranberries (3 cups), picked over**
1 **cup packed brown sugar**
½ **cup dried apricots, chopped**
½ **cup golden raisins**
¼ **cup cider vinegar**
2 **Tbsp. minced peeled fresh ginger**
1 **small onion, finely chopped**
1 **clementine or small orange, unpeeled, seeds discarded, and finely chopped**
   Salt

1. In 3-quart saucepan, combine cranberries, brown sugar, apricots, raisins, vinegar, minced ginger, onion, clementine, and ½ tsp. salt; heat to boiling on high. Reduce heat to low and simmer, uncovered, 30 minutes or until mixture thickens, stirring occasionally.

2. Spoon chutney into serving bowl; cover and refrigerate until well chilled, at least 4 hours or up to 1 week.

Brussels Sprouts with Pancetta & Rosemary

From Good Housekeeping
Prep 20 minutes
Cook 6 minutes
Makes 8 side-dish servings

    Salt and pepper
3 containers (10 oz. each) Brussels sprouts
1 Tbsp. olive oil
2 oz. pancetta, chopped (½ cup)
1 tsp. chopped fresh rosemary
¼ cup pine nuts, toasted

1. In covered 5- to 6-quart saucepot on high, heat 3 quarts water and 1 tsp. salt to boiling. Meanwhile, pull off any yellow or wilted leaves from Brussels sprouts; trim stem ends. Cut each sprout in half.

2. Add Brussels sprouts to boiling water and cook, uncovered, 5 minutes. Drain. Plunge Brussels sprouts into large bowl filled with ice water to chill quickly. Drain well. If not continuing with recipe right away, place sprouts in plastic storage bags and refrigerate until ready to use.

3. In 12-inch skillet on medium, heat oil until hot. Add pancetta and cook 2 to 3 minutes or until it begins to brown. Stir in rosemary and cook 1 minute.

4. To mixture in skillet, add Brussels sprouts and ½ tsp. each salt and freshly ground black pepper, and cook on medium-high 5 minutes or until heated through, stirring frequently. Add toasted pine nuts; toss to combine.

Sprouts Secret

For sweet, delicious sprouts, simply avoid overcooking. We briefly blanch the sprouts early in the day and sauté them to reheat and add flavorings just before serving.

Apple Cider Braised Greens
From Good Housekeeping
Prep 30 minutes **Cook** about 35 minutes **Makes** 16 side-dish servings

1½ lbs. mustard greens
1½ lbs. collard greens
1½ lbs. Swiss chard
2 Tbsp. olive oil
3 large garlic cloves, thinly sliced
1¼ cups apple cider
1 Tbsp. cider vinegar
    Salt
2 red cooking apples such as Gala or Rome Beauty, unpeeled and cut into ¾-inch chunks

1. Remove and discard stems from mustard greens. Trim stem ends from collard greens and Swiss chard; remove stems from leaves. Cut stems into 1-inch pieces; cut leaves into 2-inch pieces. Rinse and drain well.

2. In 8-quart saucepot on high, heat oil until hot. Add garlic and cook 30 seconds to 1 minute or until golden, stirring constantly. Add as many leaves and stems as possible, cider, vinegar, and 1½ tsp. salt, stirring to wilt greens. Add remaining greens in batches.

3. Reduce heat to medium. Cover saucepot and cook greens 15 minutes. Stir in apples; cook, partially covered, 10 minutes longer or until stems are very tender and most liquid evaporates, stirring occasionally. With slotted spoon, transfer greens to serving bowl.

Tarragon Peas & Pearl Onions

From Good Housekeeping **Prep** 6 minutes **Cook** 10 minutes **Makes** 8 side-dish servings

2 Tbsp. margarine or butter
1 bag (16 oz.) frozen pearl onions
1 bag (16 oz.) frozen peas
¼ cup water
Salt and pepper
1 Tbsp. fresh tarragon leaves, chopped

1. In 12-inch skillet on medium-high, heat margarine on until melted. Add frozen pearl onions, and cook 6 to 7 minutes or until browned.

2. Add frozen peas, water, ½ tsp. salt, and ¼ tsp. black pepper to skillet; stir to combine. Cover and cook 3 to 4 minutes or until onions and peas are tender.

3. Stir chopped fresh tarragon into vegetables and spoon into serving bowl.

Warm Sweet-and-Sour Orange Beets

From Redbook
Prep 20 minutes
Cook 1 hour and 10 minutes
Makes 12 side-dish servings

1½ lbs. medium red beets
  without tops, rinsed
1½ lbs. medium golden beets
  without tops, rinsed
 ¾ cup sugar
 2 Tbsp. cornstarch
 1 tsp. kosher salt
 1 cup orange juice
 ⅔ cup malt vinegar
1½ tsp. grated orange zest
 2 Tbsp. unsalted butter
 2 Tbsp. honey

1. Heat oven to 400°F. Wrap red and golden beets separately in foil packets. Roast 1 hour or until tender. Cool and peel beets; cut into ½-inch dice.

2. In a large deep skillet, mix together sugar, cornstarch, and salt; stir in orange juice and vinegar until cornstarch is dissolved. Bring mixture to a boil; reduce heat to low and simmer 5 minutes, stirring frequently, or until mixture is thick and translucent.

3. Stir in beets, orange zest, butter, and honey. Continue to simmer until beets are glossy, about 2 minutes longer.

Roasted Green Beans with Preserved Lemon & Pine Nuts

From Redbook **Prep** 30 minutes **Cook** 15 minutes **Makes** 12 side-dish servings

 2 lbs. green beans, trimmed
 ¼ cup pine nuts
 3 Tbsp. extra-virgin olive oil
 2 Tbsp. white balsamic vinegar
 4 anchovy fillets, minced,
  or 1 Tbsp. anchovy paste
 2 cloves garlic, crushed
  with press
 1 Tbsp. honey
 ¼ cup purchased preserved
  lemon, sliced into
  ½-inch strips
  Freshly ground black pepper

1. Bring a large pot of lightly salted water to a boil; add green beans and blanch 3 minutes or until bright green and crisp-tender. Drain in a colander; rinse under cold water to stop the cooking. Drain; let dry on paper towels.

2. Place nuts in a large nonstick skillet over medium heat; cook 2 minutes, tossing nuts frequently. Let cool.

3. Whisk oil, vinegar, anchovies, garlic, and honey until blended. Place green beans and preserved lemon in a shallow roasting pan; add oil mixture and toss until evenly coated. Roast 8 to 10 minutes, tossing twice, or until lightly browned and tender.

4. Transfer to a platter and season with pepper. Top green beans with toasted pine nuts.

Carrot & Parsnip Coins

From Good Housekeeping **Prep** 15 minutes **Cook** 13 minutes **Makes** 4 side-dish servings

1 navel orange
1 Tbsp. margarine or butter
¾ cup water
1 lb. medium carrots, peeled and thinly sliced
8 oz. medium parsnips, peeled and thinly sliced
¼ tsp. ground nutmeg
Salt

1. From orange, grate ½ tsp. peel and squeeze ¼ cup juice.

2. In 12-inch skillet, combine margarine, water, carrots, parsnips, ground nutmeg, and ½ tsp. salt. Cover and heat to boiling on medium-high. Reduce to medium and cook, covered, 3 minutes. Stir in orange juice and cook, uncovered, 6 to 8 minutes longer or until vegetables are tender-crisp and most liquid evaporates. Stir in orange peel.

Tasty Topping

Gremolata is an Italian garnish of lemon, parsley, and garlic that is served on anything from stews to vegetables.

Leftover Turkey

Because there's a lot of holiday bird to eat, even after the sandwiches.

Sweet & Crunchy Salad

From Redbook
Prep 15 minutes
Cook 15 minutes
Makes 4 servings

- 1 **loaf corn bread, cut into ½-inch cubes (3 cups)**
- 1 **cup (4 oz.) pecans**
- 3 **cups leftover cooked turkey, cut into ¾-inch cubes**
- ½ **cup dried cranberries**
- 12 **cups mixed greens**
- ½ **cup balsamic dressing**

1. Heat oven to 350°F. Place corn bread cubes on a baking sheet and toast until lightly browned, turning once, about 10 minutes.

2. Meanwhile, in a large skillet, toast pecans until lightly browned, about 5 minutes.

3. In a large salad bowl, toss turkey, pecans, cranberries, and greens with balsamic dressing. Add corn bread croutons and gently toss.

Steamed Broccoli with Gremolata Crumbs

From Good Housekeeping
Prep 5 minutes **Cook** 4 minutes **Makes** 4 side-dish servings

- 1 **lemon**
- 1 **bag (12 oz.) broccoli florets**
- 2 **Tbsp. water**
- 1 **tsp. olive oil**
- 1 **clove garlic, crushed with press**
- 1 **slice firm white bread, toasted and crumbled**
  Salt
- 2 **Tbsp. chopped fresh parsley leaves**

1. From lemon, grate ½ tsp. peel and squeeze 1 Tbsp. juice.

2. In microwave-safe bowl, place broccoli and water. Cover with vented plastic wrap and cook in microwave on High 4 to 5 minutes, until tender-crisp.

3. In skillet, heat oil on medium-high. Add garlic and cook 30 seconds. Stir in lemon peel, bread crumbs, and ¼ tsp. salt, and toss to combine; remove skillet from heat and stir in parsley.

4. Drain broccoli if necessary; transfer to serving bowl and toss with lemon juice. Sprinkle crumb mixture over broccoli to serve.

Holiday Desserts

End a celebratory Christmas dinner with one of our standout confections. Cakes, pies, trifle, and more—you'll treasure these special recipes for years to come.

Chocolate Peppermint Ice Cream Cake

From Redbook **Prep** 30 minutes **Cook** 14 minutes
Freeze overnight **Makes** 10 servings

CAKE
- ½ cup cake flour (not self-rising)
- ⅓ cup unsweetened cocoa powder
- ¾ tsp. baking powder
- ¼ tsp. salt
- 5 large eggs, at room temperature
- ¾ cup granulated sugar
- 1½ tsp. each vanilla and peppermint extract
  Confectioners' sugar

FILLING
- 2 pints peppermint-bark ice cream, softened

GLAZE
- ½ cup heavy cream
- 6 oz. bittersweet or semisweet chocolate, chopped
- 2 Tbsp. dark corn syrup
- 1½ tsp. each vanilla and peppermint extracts

GARNISH
- Dark and/or white chocolate curls or shavings

1. CAKE: Heat oven to 400°F. Line a 15½- by 10½- by 1-inch jelly-roll pan with nonstick foil. In a small bowl, combine cake flour, cocoa powder, baking powder, and salt.

2. Separate egg whites and yolks into 2 large bowls. Beat whites on medium-high speed until foamy. Gradually beat in ½ cup of the sugar. Continue to beat on high speed just until stiff (but not dry) peaks form.

3. Using same beaters, beat yolks with the remaining ¼ cup sugar and extracts until thickened, about 3 minutes. On low speed, beat in flour mixture until blended. Stir in one-quarter of beaten egg whites into mixture. Fold in remaining whites. Spread in prepared pan; smooth top. Bake 12 minutes or until top springs back when gently pressed. Let cool 2 minutes on a wire rack.

4. Dust a clean towel with confectioners' sugar; invert cake onto towel. Remove pan; carefully peel off foil. Starting from the short end, roll up cake in towel; place seam side down on wire rack; cool completely.

5. FILLING: Unroll cake and spread evenly with ice cream. Roll up cake. Wrap tightly in nonstick foil and freeze, seam side down, overnight until firm.

6. GLAZE: In a small saucepan, heat cream, chocolate, and corn syrup over low heat until chocolate is melted and glaze is shiny and smooth, 1 to 2 minutes. Stir in extracts; cool to room temperature.

7. Unwrap cake; trim ends. Place cake on a wire rack over waxed paper. Pour glaze along top of cake roll, spreading with a spatula to cover sides. Garnish top of cake with chocolate curls or shavings. Freeze cake until firm.

Chocolate Soufflé From Good Housekeeping **Prep** 10 minutes **Cook** 15 minutes **Makes** 4 servings

Nonstick baking spray with flour

4 **oz. bittersweet chocolate chips (scant 1 cup)**

⅓ **cup sweetened condensed milk**

3 **large eggs, separated**

2 **Tbsp. confectioners' sugar**

1. Preheat oven to 375°F. Generously coat four 4-ounce ceramic or glass ramekins with nonstick baking spray with flour.

2. In microwave-safe large bowl, microwave chocolate chips on High in 20-second increments, stirring, until just melted (1 to 2 minutes). Remove from microwave; with wire whisk, whisk in condensed milk. Whisk in 2 egg yolks until blended; refrigerate remaining egg yolk for another use.

3. In another large bowl, with mixer on medium speed, beat egg whites until medium-stiff peaks form (3 to 4 minutes). Add one-third of beaten whites to chocolate mixture, and whisk gently until incorporated. With rubber spatula, gently fold in remaining whites until just incorporated. Divide batter among prepared ramekins. If preparing ahead of time, cover with plastic wrap and refrigerate until ready to bake. (Remove plastic wrap before baking.)

4. Sift confectioners' sugar over tops. Place ramekins in jelly-roll pan for easier handling. Bake 11 to 13 minutes or until tops rise about 1 inch above rim; do not open oven while baking. Serve immediately.

Fast and Fab
This recipe takes less than half the time of a traditional soufflé, and is every bit as impressive.

Peppermint-Chocolate Layer Cake
From Good Housekeeping

Prep 35 minutes plus chilling and setting **Cook** 40 minutes **Makes** 12 servings

ONE-BOWL CHOCOLATE CAKE

- 2 **cups all-purpose flour**
- 1½ **cups sugar**
- ¾ **cup unsweetened cocoa**
- 1 **tsp. baking soda**
- 1 **tsp. baking powder**
- ½ **tsp. salt**
- ¾ **cup hot water**
- ¾ **cup low-fat buttermilk**
- ½ **cup vegetable oil**
- 3 **large. eggs**
- 1 **tsp. pure vanilla extract**

CHOCOLATE GANACHE FROSTING AND GLAZE

- 1 **lb. semisweet chocolate, finely chopped**
- 1½ **cups heavy or whipping cream**
- 1 **tsp. peppermint extract**
- 14 **dark chocolate thin mint candies**
- 1 **Tbsp. corn syrup**
  Candy canes, peppermint sticks, and starlight mints, for decorating

1. PREPARE CAKE: Preheat oven to 350°F. Lightly grease two 9-inch round cake pans. Line bottoms with parchment paper; lightly grease paper.

2. In large bowl, with mixer on low speed, beat flour, sugar, cocoa, baking soda, baking powder, and salt until well combined. With mixer running, add water, buttermilk, oil, eggs, and vanilla. Increase speed to medium and beat until smooth, scraping bowl occasionally. Divide batter between prepared pans.

3. Bake 25 to 30 minutes or until toothpick inserted in centers comes out clean. Let cool in pans on wire racks 10 minutes. Invert onto racks. Discard parchment paper; cool completely. Cake layers can be kept at room temperature, wrapped tightly in plastic wrap, overnight.

4. PREPARE GANACHE: Place chocolate in large heatproof bowl. In 2-quart saucepan, heat cream on medium-high until just bubbling. Immediately pour over chocolate. Let stand 1 minute, then stir until smooth. Stir in peppermint extract until well incorporated. Return one-third ganache (about 1 cup) to saucepan; set aside for glaze. Refrigerate remaining ganache, uncovered, 10 minutes; with wire whisk, stir well. Repeat chilling and stirring until ganache is the consistency of frosting and becomes light brown.

5. With long serrated knife, cut each cake in half horizontally. Place 1 layer, cut side up, on wire rack set over waxed paper. Spread top with one-quarter of frosting and top with another cake layer, cut side up. Spread with another quarter of frosting and top with even layer of thin mint candies, breaking pieces to fit. Place another cake layer on top. Spread with another quarter of frosting and top with final cake layer. Spread remaining frosting over top and sides of cake to seal in crumbs. Let stand in cool place for frosting to harden and set.

6. When frosting is set, add corn syrup to reserved ganache in saucepan. Heat on low just until runny, stirring constantly. Pour glaze over cake and immediately spread to evenly coat top and sides. (Excess glaze will run through rack.) Let cake stand until set. Carefully transfer to cake plate. Decorate with candy as desired.

THE SWEET SURPRISE
in the middle of this candy-embellished cake:
a layer of chocolate mints

Chocolate Gingerbread Cake From Good Housekeeping
Prep 25 minutes plus cooling **Cook** 1 hour **Makes** 12 servings

- 2 cups all-purpose flour
- ¾ cup unsweetened cocoa
- 1½ tsp. ground ginger
- 1½ tsp. baking powder
- ½ tsp. baking soda
- ¼ tsp. salt
- ¾ cup butter (1½ sticks), softened, no substitutions
- ¾ cup packed brown sugar
- ¾ cup granulated sugar
- 1 Tbsp. grated peeled fresh ginger
- 3 large eggs
- ¼ cup blackstrap molasses
- 1 cup low-fat buttermilk
- 2 cups semisweet chocolate chips
- 1 Tbsp. confectioners' sugar, for dusting

1. Preheat oven to 325°F. Coat 12-cup decorative tree Bundt pan with nonstick baking spray.

2. On sheet of waxed paper, sift together flour, cocoa, ground ginger, baking powder, baking soda, and salt.

3. In large bowl, with mixer on medium-high speed, beat butter and sugars until creamy. Beat in fresh ginger. Reduce speed to medium; beat in eggs, 1 at a time, then molasses, scraping bowl occasionally with rubber spatula.

4. Add flour mixture alternately with buttermilk, beginning and ending with flour mixture. Beat just until combined, scraping bowl occasionally with rubber spatula. Fold in chocolate chips.

5. Pour batter into prepared pan. Bake 1 hour or until toothpick inserted in center of cake comes out clean. Cool in pan on wire rack 10 minutes. Invert onto wire rack and carefully remove pan. Cool completely on wire rack.

6. Before serving, dust with confectioners' sugar.

Nordic Noël
A dusting of powdered sugar subs for just-fallen snow in this forest of Chocolate Gingerbread Cake.

Cranberry Trifle From Good Housekeeping

Prep 30 minutes plus chilling **Cook** about 20 minutes **Makes** 12 servings

- 2 navel oranges
- 1 bag (12 oz.) fresh cranberries (about 3 cups)
- 1¼ cups water
- 1 cup sugar
- 2 Tbsp. chopped crystallized ginger (¾ oz.)
- ¼ tsp. ground cinnamon
- ⅛ tsp. ground allspice
- 1 cup heavy or whipping cream
- 1 package instant vanilla pudding and pie filling for 4 servings
- 2 cups milk
- 1 frozen pound cake (16 oz.), cut into ¾-inch cubes

1. From oranges, grate 1 tsp. peel and place in 4-quart saucepan. With knife, remove all remaining peel and white pith from oranges. Holding 1 orange at a time over same saucepan, to catch juice, cut sections from between membranes and add to saucepan, then squeeze juice from membranes into saucepan; discard membranes.

2. Set aside a few cranberries for garnish. In same saucepan, stir remaining cranberries with water, sugar, ginger, cinnamon, and allspice. Heat to boiling over high heat, stirring often. Reduce heat to medium and cook 15 to 17 minutes or until cranberries pop and sauce thickens slightly, stirring occasionally. Remove from heat; cool to room temperature.

3. Meanwhile, in bowl, with mixer on medium speed, beat cream until soft peaks form. In large bowl, with whisk, prepare pudding with milk as label directs. Immediately fold whipped cream into pudding until blended.

4. In 3-quart glass trifle bowl or other serving bowl, place one-third of cake. Spoon one-third of cranberry mixture over cake, spreading to side of bowl. Top with one-third of pudding. Repeat layering 2 more times. Garnish with reserved cranberries.

5. Cover trifle and refrigerate at least 4 hours or up to 2 days.

Leftover Cranberries?

Put them to use in one of these recipes for the holidays—or after.

LINZER WAFFLE SUNDAES

In microwave-safe 2-quart bowl, combine 2 cups **cranberries**, ⅔ cup packed **brown sugar**, 2 Tbsp. **water**, and ¼ tsp. **ground cinnamon**. Cover with vented plastic wrap, and microwave on High 3 minutes or until berries begin to pop. Toast 4 frozen **Belgian waffles**. Top waffles with 1 pint **vanilla ice cream**, then cranberry sauce.

CRANBERRY COFFEE CAKE

Preheat oven to 400°F. In 9- by 9-inch metal baking pan, melt 5 Tbsp. **butter or margarine** in oven. Spoon 3 Tbsp. butter from pan into bowl; whisk in ¾ cup **water**, ½ cup **sugar**, and 2 large **eggs**. Stir in 2½ cups **reduced-fat baking mix** until combined. Top butter remaining in pan with 1 bag (12 oz.) **cranberries**; sprinkle with ⅔ cup **sugar**. Spread batter over ingredients in pan. Bake 35 to 40 minutes. Cool cake 25 minutes, then loosen edges with knife and invert onto plate.

ROSEMARY-CRANBERRY SORBET

In a pot over high heat, bring ½ cup **sugar**, ½ cup **water**, and 2 sprigs **rosemary** to boil. Remove from heat and let steep for 45 minutes, until syrup forms. In a blender or food processor, puree one 16-oz. can **whole-berry cranberry sauce**; 2 peeled, cored, and chopped crisp **apples**; juice of 1 large **lemon**; and **rosemary syrup**. Finely strain mixture and chill for 1 hour. Freeze in an ice-cream maker according to manufacturer instructions. Transfer to a chilled bowl, cover with plastic wrap, and freeze until firm, about 1 hour.

Cranberry-Orange Cheesecake

From Redbook **Prep** 25 minutes **Cook** 1 hour and 14 minutes **Makes** 16 servings

CRUST

- 1½ cups graham cracker crumbs
- 3 Tbsp. light brown sugar
- ¼ tsp. ground cinnamon
- 4 Tbsp. unsalted butter, melted

FILLING

- 3 (8 oz.) packages cream cheese, softened
- 1 cup granulated sugar
- 1½ Tbsp. all-purpose flour
- ¾ cup sour cream
- 3 large eggs
- 2 tsp. grated orange zest
- 1 tsp. vanilla extract

SOUR CREAM TOPPING

- 1¼ cups sour cream
- ¼ cup granulated sugar
- 1 Tbsp. orange juice

CRANBERRY TOPPING

- 1½ cups granulated sugar
- ⅓ cup each orange juice and light corn syrup
- 4 cups fresh cranberries
- 1 tsp. grated orange zest

1. CRUST: Lightly coat a 9-inch springform pan with cooking spray. In a bowl, combine crust ingredients until moistened; press mixture onto bottom and halfway up sides of pan. Heat oven to 350°F.

2. FILLING: In a bowl, with mixer at medium speed, beat cream cheese just until smooth; slowly beat in sugar, scraping bowl often with rubber spatula. Beat in flour, then remaining filling ingredients. Beat 3 minutes, occasionally scraping bowl. Pour into crust. Bake cheesecake 1 hour, or until set but slightly jiggly in center.

3. SOUR CREAM TOPPING: Whisk together the sour cream topping ingredients until smooth; remove cheesecake from oven and spread over top of cake. Return cheesecake to oven and bake 10 minutes longer, until set. Remove from oven and cool completely in pan on wire rack. Cover and refrigerate until well chilled.

4. CRANBERRY TOPPING: In a medium saucepan, bring sugar, orange juice, and corn syrup to a boil, stirring to dissolve sugar. Add cranberries and cook 4 minutes, or until skins split. Remove from heat; stir in zest. Cool mixture completely. Cover and refrigerate up to 2 days ahead.

5. With spatula, loosen pan side from cheesecake and remove. Loosen cake from pan bottom; slide onto plate. Spoon cranberry topping over cheesecake.

Ready, Set, Start!

You can prepare the crust through step 3 and freeze it, unbaked, up to one month ahead. Or prepare and prebake the crust through step 4 up to one day ahead. The cranberry topping in step 7 can keep in the refrigerator up to three days but should be brought to room temperature before using. The almond filling will taste best if prepared on the morning of the party.

Cranberry-Almond Pie

From Good Housekeeping **Prep** 30 minutes **Cook** 1 hour **Makes** 12 servings

BAKED PIE SHELL

- 1⅓ cups all-purpose flour
- ¼ tsp. salt
- 5 Tbsp. cold butter or margarine, cut up
- 3 Tbsp. vegetable shortening
- 4 to 5 Tbsp. ice water

ALMOND FILLING

- 1 tube (7 oz.) or can (8 oz.) almond paste
- 4 Tbsp. butter or margarine, softened
- ½ cup sugar
- 3 large eggs
- ¼ cup all-purpose flour
  Pinch salt

CRANBERRY TOPPING

- 1 bag (12 oz.) cranberries (3 cups)
- ⅔ cup sugar
- ⅓ cup water
- ½ tsp. grated fresh orange peel plus additional for garnish

1. BAKED PIE SHELL: In food processor with knife blade attached, pulse flour and salt until well blended. Add cold butter and shortening, and pulse just until mixture resembles coarse crumbs. Sprinkle in ice water, 1 Tbsp. at a time, pulsing after each addition, just until large moist crumbs begin to form.

2. With hands, shape dough into disk; wrap in plastic wrap and refrigerate 30 minutes or overnight. (If chilled overnight, let dough stand 30 minutes at room temperature before rolling to prevent cracking.)

3. Preheat oven to 425°F. On lightly floured surface, with floured rolling pin, roll dough into 12-inch round. Ease dough into 9-inch glass or ceramic pie plate. Gently press dough against bottom and up sides of plate without stretching. Trim dough edge, leaving 1-inch overhang. Fold overhang under; pinch to form stand-up edge, then make decorative edge. Freeze pie shell 15 minutes.

4. Line pie shell with foil or parchment paper, and fill with pie weights, dried beans, or uncooked rice. Bake 10 to 12 minutes or until beginning to set. Remove foil with weights, and bake 13 to 15 minutes longer or until golden. If shell puffs during baking, gently press it down with back of spoon. Cool on wire rack at least 10 minutes. Reset oven control to 350°F.

5. ALMOND FILLING: In food processor with knife blade attached, blend almond paste, softened butter, and sugar until smooth. Add eggs, flour, and salt; blend until well mixed, occasionally scraping down side of processor bowl with rubber spatula.

6. Fill pie shell with almond filling. Bake 30 to 33 minutes or until filling is slightly puffed and golden. Cool completely on wire rack, about 3 hours.

7. CRANBERRY TOPPING: While pie is baking and cooling, in 2-quart saucepan, combine 1½ cups cranberries with sugar, water, and ½ tsp. orange peel; heat to boiling over high heat. Reduce heat to medium-low; simmer 5 minutes or until mixture thickens slightly and most cranberries have popped, stirring occasionally. Stir in remaining cranberries. Set cranberry topping aside to cool to room temperature.

8. To serve, spoon cranberry topping over almond filling just before serving; garnish with orange peel. Refrigerate any leftovers up to 4 days.

Make It Special
3 Perfect Crusts

These fancy, fluted edges are easier to create than you may think.

CRIMPED Push one index finger against outer edge of rim between the index finger and thumb of other hand, as shown; pinch to make crimp. Repeat.

FORKED Fold overhanging dough under and press edge to lie flat. With floured fork, press dough to rim of plate; repeat around edge.

TURRET With kitchen shears, make cuts, ½ inch apart, around edge of crust. Fold cut sections alternately toward center and toward rim.

Go Nuts!
Put pecans in a 350°F. oven for 10 minutes before adding to the filling. They'll be nuttier and crunchier.

Taste Test
Prepared Pie Crust

You don't have to make your own pie crust to serve great pie.

When you're busy with turkey, stuffing, and all the fixings, you may not feel up to making your own pastry. But what would the holidays be without pie? Fortunately, prepared pie crusts can save you time, and, just as important, they taste like homemade. Many even come in their own pie tins (hooray—one less dish to wash on the holiday!). We searched for the best ones and sampled—with and without filling—the frozen, pre-rolled refrigerated, and dry-mix varieties of crust to test flavor, flakiness, and durability when filled. These winners can make your holiday dinner easy as pie:

FIRST PLACE

By far the flakiest contender, Wholly Wholesome Organic Traditional 9" Pie Shells won for their natural, buttery flavor—they taste just like Grandma's.

HONORABLE MENTION

The classic blue box of Jiffy Pie Crust Mix produced crisp, crumbly crusts with a good balance of salty and sweet—all for less than a dollar.

Old-Fashioned Pecan Pie From Good Housekeeping

Prep 23 minutes **Cook** 45 minutes **Makes** 10 servings

- **9-inch prepared pie shell**
- ¾ **cup dark corn syrup**
- ½ **cup packed dark brown sugar**
- 3 **Tbsp. butter or margarine, melted**
- 1 **tsp. vanilla extract**
  Pinch salt
- 3 **large eggs**
- 1½ **cups pecan halves, toasted**

1. Bake prepared pie shell. Cool pie shell on wire rack at least 10 minutes. Reset oven to 350°F.

2. In large bowl, with wire whisk, mix corn syrup, sugar, butter, vanilla, salt, and eggs until blended. With spoon, stir in pecans.

3. Pour the filling into pie shell. Bake 43 to 45 minutes or until filling is set around edge but center still jiggles slightly. Cool pie on wire rack at least 3 hours for easier slicing. Refrigerate leftovers up to 1 week.

Dark Chocolate–Walnut Caramel Pie From Good Housekeeping
Prep 25 minutes **Cook** 40 minutes plus chilling and cooling **Makes** 12 servings

9-inch prepared pie shell
- 1 **cup sugar**
- ¼ **cup water**
- 1¼ **cups heavy or whipping cream**
- 8 **oz. semisweet chocolate, cut up**
- 2 **Tbsp. butter or margarine**
- 2 **tsp. vanilla extract**
- 1¾ **cups walnuts, toasted and coarsely chopped**

1. Bake prepared pie shell. Cool pie shell on wire rack at least 15 minutes.

2. In heavy 3-quart saucepan, heat sugar and water over medium-high until sugar dissolves and turns amber in color, 15 minutes, swirling pan occasionally.

3. Meanwhile, in microwave-safe 1-cup liquid measuring cup, heat ¾ cup cream in microwave on High 45 seconds or until warm. Place remaining ½ cup cream in refrigerator to keep cold for whipping later.

4. Remove saucepan from heat. Stir in warm cream until a smooth caramel forms (caramel will stiffen when cream is added). Stir in chocolate and butter until completely melted. Stir in vanilla extract and 1½ cups walnuts. Reserve remaining ¼ cup walnuts to sprinkle on top of pie later.

5. Pour warm chocolate filling into pie shell. Cool 1 hour on wire rack, then cover and refrigerate at least 3 hours or until set.

6. When ready to serve, in medium bowl, with mixer on medium speed, beat remaining ½ cup heavy cream until soft peaks form. With metal spatula, spread whipped cream on top of pie, being careful to leave a ½-inch border all around the edges. Sprinkle pie with reserved walnuts.

Double-Crust Apple Pie

From Good Housekeeping **Prep** 50 minutes **Cook** 1 hour 10 minutes **Makes** 10 servings

PASTRY

- 2½ **cups all-purpose flour**
- ½ **tsp. salt**
- 10 **Tbsp. cold butter or margarine, cut up**
- 6 **Tbsp. vegetable shortening**
- 6 to 7 **Tbsp. ice water**

APPLE FILLING

- ⅔ **cup sugar**
- ⅓ **cup cornstarch**
- ½ **tsp. ground cinnamon**
- ¼ **tsp. ground nutmeg**
- ¼ **tsp. salt**
- 3½ **lbs. Granny Smith, Golden Delicious, and/or Braeburn apples, each peeled, cored, and cut into 16 wedges**
- 1 **Tbsp. fresh lemon juice**
- 2 **Tbsp. butter or margarine, cut up**
- 1 **large egg white, lightly beaten**
- 1 **tsp. sugar**

1. PASTRY: In food processor with knife blade attached, blend flour and salt. Add butter and shortening, and pulse until mixture resembles coarse crumbs. Sprinkle in ice water, 1 Tbsp. at a time, pulsing after each addition, until large moist crumbs just begin to form.

2. Shape dough into 2 balls, 1 slightly larger. Flatten each into a disk; wrap each in plastic wrap and refrigerate 30 minutes or overnight. (If chilled overnight, let stand 30 minutes at room temperature before rolling.)

3. Meanwhile, preheat oven to 400°F. Place cookie sheet on rack in lower third of preheating oven to bake pie on later.

4. APPLE FILLING: In large bowl, combine sugar with cornstarch, cinnamon, nutmeg, and salt. Add apples and lemon juice, and toss to coat evenly.

5. On lightly floured surface, with floured rolling pin, roll larger disk of dough into 12-inch round. Ease dough into 9½-inch deep-dish glass or ceramic pie plate. Gently press dough against bottom and up side of plate without stretching. Trim dough edge, leaving 1-inch overhang; reserve trimmings. Spoon apple mixture into pie crust; dot with butter.

6. Roll remaining disk for top crust into 12-inch round. Center round over filling in bottom crust. Trim pastry edge, leaving 1-inch overhang; reserve trimmings. Fold overhang under; bring up over pie-plate rim and pinch to form stand-up edge, then make decorative edge. (See "3 Perfect Crusts," page 93.)

Brush crust with some egg white. Reroll trimmings. With knife or cookie cutters, cut out apple and/or leaf shapes; arrange on pie. Cut short slashes in round to allow steam to escape during baking. Brush cutouts with egg white; sprinkle crust and cutouts with sugar.

7. Bake pie 1 hour 10 minutes or until apples are tender when pierced with knife through slits in crust. To prevent over-browning, cover pie loosely with tent of foil after 40 minutes. Cool pie on wire rack 3 hours to serve warm. Or cool completely to serve later.

Perfect for Pie
Pick Your Apple

Some apples have the right flavor and crunch for snacking. Others keep their shape when they're heated and are ideal for baking, like these:

Cameo Extra-crunchy with a sweet-tart flavor; holds its shape under heat.

Pippin An antique American apple; considered one of the best for desserts.

Granny Smith Crisp, juicy and tart; perfect for baking, stewing, or eating out of hand.

Jonathan A sweet-tart all-purpose apple with a firm texture excellent for cooking.

Rome Beauty Superb cooking apple; retains its shape and mildly tart flavor.

Golden Delicious Great for eating fresh, or for using in pies and applesauce.

Very Merry!

Thanks to delicious cocoa and rich cream cheese frosting, red velvet desserts have become a popular trend. We think their crimson shade makes them perfect for serving during the holiday season.

3. In a 2-cup glass measuring cup, stir together buttermilk, food coloring, vinegar, vanilla, and baking soda.

4. In a large bowl with an electric mixer, beat butter and sugar on medium-high until light and fluffy. Beat in eggs, one at a time, until well blended. Beat in flour mixture alternately with buttermilk mixture on medium-low speed. Pour batter into prepared pans. Bake 25 to 30 minutes or until cake tester inserted in center comes out clean. Cool in pans on a wire rack 10 minutes. Invert onto wire rack; invert again and let cool completely on rack.

5. FROSTING: Place white chocolate and cream in a small microwave-safe bowl. Microwave on High 15 to 30 seconds; whisk until smooth. Let stand 2 minutes; cover with plastic wrap and chill.

6. In a large bowl with an electric mixer, beat cream cheese, butter, and vanilla on medium-high speed until light and fluffy, about 2 minutes. Beat in cooled white-chocolate mixture until blended. On low speed, add confectioners' sugar in batches and beat until combined. Increase speed to medium-high and beat until fluffy, about 1 minute.

7. To assemble: Cut each cake layer horizontally with a long serrated knife, to make 4 layers. Place 1 layer on a serving plate and spread with about 1 cup of frosting. Repeat with remaining 3 layers, frosting the top and sides of the cake. Sprinkle coconut on top and sides of cake. Refrigerate cake about 1 hour to let it set.

Red Velvet Snowball Cake

From Redbook **Prep** 30 minutes **Cook** 30 minutes **Makes** 16 servings

CAKE

- 2½ **cups cake flour (not self-rising)**
- ¼ **cup unsweetened cocoa powder**
- 1 **oz. grated bittersweet or semisweet chocolate**
- 1 **tsp. baking powder**
- ½ **tsp. salt**
- 1 **cup buttermilk**
- 1 **bottle (1 oz.) red food coloring**
- 2 **tsp. distilled white vinegar**
- 1 **tsp. each vanilla extract and baking soda**
- ½ **cup (1 stick) unsalted butter, softened**
- 1½ **cups sugar**
- 2 **large eggs**

FROSTING

- 4 **oz. white chocolate, chopped**
- ¼ **cup heavy cream**
- 2 **packages (8 oz.) cream cheese, softened**
- ½ **cup unsalted butter, softened**
- 1 **Tbsp. vanilla extract**
- 2½ **cups confectioners' sugar**
- 1½ **cups shredded coconut**

1. CAKE: Heat oven to 350°F. Grease two 9-inch round cake pans with baking spray. Line bottom of pans with waxed paper; spray paper with baking spray. Dust with flour; tap out excess.

2. In a medium bowl, combine flour, cocoa powder, grated chocolate, baking powder, and salt.

Red Velvet Cupcakes with Creole Cream Cheese Frosting

From Redbook **Prep** 10 minutes **Cook** 22 minutes **Makes** 12 cupcakes

CUPCAKES

- 1⅓ cups all-purpose flour
- 2 Tbsp. unsweetened cocoa powder
- ¾ tsp. baking powder
- ¼ tsp each baking soda and salt
- ½ cup (1 stick) unsalted butter, softened
- ¾ cup sugar
- 2 large eggs
- ½ cup buttermilk
- 1 Tbsp. red food coloring
- 1 tsp. vanilla extract
- ½ tsp. white vinegar

FROSTING

- 8 oz. Creole cream cheese, softened, or use 1 package (8 oz.) softened cream cheese with 1 tsp. lemon juice stirred in
- 4 Tbsp. unsalted butter, softened
- 1½ cups confectioners' sugar, sifted
- ½ tsp. vanilla extract

1. CUPCAKES: Heat oven to 350°F. Line 12-cup muffin pan with paper liners. In a small bowl, whisk flour, cocoa, baking powder, baking soda, and salt. In a large bowl, with mixer on medium speed, beat butter and sugar until light and creamy. Beat in eggs, one at a time. In a glass measure, combine buttermilk, food coloring, vanilla, and vinegar. With mixer on low speed, beat in flour mixture in thirds, alternating with buttermilk mixture, until blended. Beat 2 minutes, scraping bowl occasionally, until batter is smooth. Divide batter evenly among muffin cups.

2. Bake 18 to 22 minutes, until a pick inserted into cupcakes comes out clean. Let cool in pan 5 minutes before removing to a wire rack to cool.

3. FROSTING: In a large bowl, with electric mixer on medium speed, beat cream cheese and butter until well blended. Add confectioners' sugar and vanilla, and beat until smooth and fluffy. Frost cupcakes and refrigerate to firm up frosting. Bring cupcakes to room temperature before serving.

Super Fast, Super Good

These jelly donuts, served during Hanukkah, are baked, not fried, so they're lighter and easier to make than the traditional variety.

Sufganiyot

From Good Housekeeping **Prep** 30 minutes
Cook 15 minutes **Makes** 16 donuts

- 3 cups all-purpose flour
- ¼ cup granulated sugar
- 5 tsp. rapid-rise yeast (2 packages)
- 1 tsp. ground cinnamon
- 1 tsp. salt
- ¼ cup vegetable oil
- ¾ cup warm whole milk (120° to 130°F.), plus extra for brushing
- 2 large eggs, at room temperature
- 1 cup sour cherry or other jam
- 2 Tbsp. confectioners' sugar

1. In electric stand mixer bowl, combine flour, granulated sugar, yeast, cinnamon, and salt. With paddle attachment of stand mixer, mix on low 15 seconds or until combined. Add oil and milk; beat on medium-low speed 3 to 5 minutes or until well combined. Add eggs, one at a time; beat 10 minutes or until dough is elastic, occasionally scraping sides of bowl.

2. Meanwhile, lightly oil large bowl.

Transfer dough to prepared bowl; cover loosely with plastic wrap. Let rise 40 minutes or until doubled in bulk.

3. Lightly grease 3 cookie sheets. Gently punch down dough, folding it onto itself. On lightly oiled work surface, gently roll dough into 16-inch log; cut log crosswise into 1-inch pieces. Shape each piece into ball; transfer to prepared cookie sheets, 3 inches apart. Cover loosely with lightly oiled plastic wrap; let rise 20 to 30 minutes or until slightly puffed.

4. Preheat oven to 350°F. Brush tops of dough with milk. Bake, 1 sheet at a time, 12 to 15 minutes or until pale golden. Cool on sheets on wire racks 5 minutes.

5. Cut 1 corner of self-sealing plastic bag to make ¼-inch-diameter hole; fit with ¼- to ½-inch plain piping tip, and fill bag with jam. Slide paring knife into center of side of 1 donut without cutting through other side. Using sawing motion, cut pocket in donut without cutting opening any wider. Fit piping tip into hole, and pipe jam until filled. Repeat. Dust donuts with confectioners' sugar to serve.

Raspberry Linzer Tart

From Redbook
Prep 1 hour
Cook 50 minutes
Makes 10 servings

- 1½ cups all-purpose flour
- ¾ cup toasted sliced almonds
- ⅔ cup confectioners' sugar, plus extra for dusting
- ¾ tsp. each unsweetened cocoa powder and ground cinnamon
- ½ tsp. ground ginger
- 1¼ tsp. salt
- ⅛ tsp. ground cloves
- ½ cup (1 stick) unsalted butter, cut into small pieces
- 1½ tsp. grated lemon zest Yolks from 2 large eggs
- 1 Tbsp. water
- 1 tsp. vanilla extract
- 1 (18 oz.) jar red raspberry preserves with seeds (1⅓ cups)

1. In food processor, process flour, almonds, sugar, cocoa, cinnamon, ginger, salt, and cloves, until nuts are finely ground. Add butter and 1 tsp. of the lemon zest; pulse until crumbly. In cup with fork, mix egg yolks, water, and vanilla; add to flour mixture. Process until mixture clumps together. Turn out and press together to form dough.

2. With floured hands, pat one-third of pastry into a round, ½-inch-thick disk. Place between 2 sheets of wax paper; on baking sheet, roll to a 9-inch round and chill 30 minutes. Press remaining pastry over bottom and sides of 9-inch tart pan with removable bottom. Chill 30 minutes. Heat oven to 350°F.

3. Remove top paper from pastry round; with fluted or regular pastry wheel, cut into 14 (½-inch-wide) strips. Arrange strips in lattice on baking sheet; freeze until firm enough to lift without breaking. Stir remaining ½ tsp. lemon zest into preserves; spread evenly into tart crust in pan. Cover with lattice; trim to edge of pan.

4. Bake 50 minutes, or until brown. Cool completely on wire rack. Remove sides of tart pan. Dust top of tart with confectioners' sugar.

Impress
your guests!

Spicy ginger is one of the traditional flavors of the season. Savor it in either of these standout desserts, which are perfect for company and special holiday dinners.

Gingered Carrot Cake with Cream Cheese Frosting

From Good Housekeeping **Prep** 1 hour plus cooling
Cook 35 minutes **Makes** 20 servings

CAKE

- 2½ cups all-purpose flour
- 2 tsp. baking soda
- 2 tsp. ground cinnamon
- 1 tsp. baking powder
- 1 tsp. ground ginger
- ½ tsp. ground nutmeg
  Salt
- 4 large eggs
- 1 cup butter or margarine
  (2 sticks), softened
- ¾ cup granulated sugar
- ¾ cup packed light brown sugar
- 1 can (8 oz.) crushed pineapple in
  unsweetened juice
- 1 Tbsp. vanilla extract
- 3⅓ cups shredded carrots
  (about 1 lb.)
- 1 cup walnuts, coarsely chopped
  (4 oz.)
- ¾ cup raisins
- ¼ cup finely chopped crystallized
  ginger (about 1½ oz.)

FROSTING

- 6 oz. cream cheese, softened
- 3 Tbsp. butter, softened
  (no substitutions)
- 2 tsp. vanilla extract
- 2¼ cups confectioners' sugar
  Chopped crystallized ginger
  for garnish

1. CAKE: Preheat oven to 350°F. Grease two 9-inch round cake pans; dust with flour.

2. On waxed paper, combine flour, baking soda, cinnamon, baking powder, ground ginger, nutmeg, and 1 tsp. salt.

3. In large bowl, with mixer on medium speed, beat eggs, butter, and sugars 2 minutes, occasionally scraping bowl with rubber spatula. Beat in pineapple with its juice and vanilla. Reduce speed to low; add flour mixture and beat just until blended. Stir in carrots, walnuts, raisins, and crystallized ginger.

4. Spoon batter evenly into prepared pans. Bake 32 to 35 minutes or until toothpick inserted in center comes out almost clean. Cool in pans on wire rack 15 minutes. With thin knife, loosen sides of cakes from pans; invert onto racks and let cool.

5. Assemble cake: Place 1 cake layer, rounded side down, on cake plate. With narrow metal spatula, spread 1 cup frosting (see below) over layer. Top with second layer, rounded side up. Spread remaining frosting on top of cake. If you like, sprinkle crystallized ginger on top of cake for garnish. If not serving cake right away, cover loosely with plastic wrap and refrigerate up to 2 days.

6. FROSTING: In large bowl, with mixer on low speed, beat cream cheese, butter, and vanilla until blended. Increase speed to medium-high; beat 2 minutes or until very fluffy. Reduce speed to low; add confectioners' sugar and beat 2 minutes or until smooth. Makes about 1¾ cups.

Upside-Down Quince Gingerbread Cake

From Redbook **Prep** 15 minutes **Cook** 58 minutes **Makes** 8 servings

- ¾ cup sugar
- ¼ cup water
- ¼ cup (½ stick) unsalted butter
- 4 ripe quinces or tart apples
  (2 lbs.), peeled, cored, and cut
  into ½-inch-thick wedges
- 1 box (14 oz.) gingerbread mix
- 1¼ cups buttermilk
  Vanilla ice cream

1. Heat oven to 350°F. Coat a 9- by 2-inch round cake pan with cooking spray.

2. Mix sugar and water in a large skillet; bring to a boil over medium-high heat. Boil mixture 3 to 4 minutes, or until a light honey color. Add butter and reduce heat to medium; when butter is melted, boil mixture 1 minute, until light

golden. Add quinces and cook 8 minutes, turning quinces several times, until lightly caramelized and crisp-tender when pierced with the tip of a knife. Remove from heat; cool in skillet 5 minutes. Pour quince mixture into prepared baking pan so slices cover bottom of pan evenly.

3. Using an electric beater, beat gingerbread mix with buttermilk until batter is smooth. Pour over quinces and carefully spread to edges of pan. Bake 40 to 45 minutes, until a pick inserted in center comes out clean.

4. Cool cake in pan on a wire rack 15 minutes. Invert onto a serving plate. Cool until cake is just warm (this cake is also delicious at room temperature). Serve with vanilla ice cream.

What Is a Quince?

A relative of the apple and pear, quince turns a bright golden yellow when it ripens in the fall. It is popular in Spain and Latin America.

Gourmet Marshmallows From Country Living

Prep 40 minutes plus resting **Cook** 15 minutes **Makes** 12 marshmallows per flavor

- ¼ **cup confectioners' sugar**
- ¼ **cup cornstarch**
  Vegetable oil, for pan
- 2 **(¼-oz.) envelopes unflavored gelatin**
- 1½ **cups granulated sugar**
- ⅔ **cup light corn syrup**

1. In a small bowl, sift together confectioners' sugar and cornstarch; set aside. Brush the bottom and sides of an 8-inch-square baking pan with vegetable oil. Cut an 8- by 12-inch sheet of parchment and fit into pan so that it covers bottom and 2 sides. Brush parchment with oil, and coat parchment and pan with half of the confectioners' sugar mixture. Set aside.

2. Fill a large bowl with ½ cup cool water and sprinkle with gelatin; set aside. In a medium pot fitted with a candy thermometer, combine granulated sugar, corn syrup, and ½ cup water; bring to a boil over high heat. Reduce heat to medium and cook until mixture reaches 240°F., 7 to 10 minutes. Remove from heat and set aside.

3. Using an electric mixer, beat reserved gelatin mixture on low for about 30 seconds, then pour in reserved sugar–corn syrup mixture in a slow, steady stream down side of bowl. Increase mixer speed to high and beat until very thick, ribbony, and doubled in volume, 12 to 15 minutes.

4. Pour batter into prepared pan. Using dampened fingers, smooth top. Sprinkle remaining confectioners' sugar mixture over top. Let rest, uncovered, in a cool, dry place, about 4 hours or up to overnight.

5. Invert marshmallow onto a dry surface and discard parchment. Using a clean, dry pastry brush, dust excess confectioners' sugar from the top of the marshmallow onto work surface. Dust a knife in confectioners' sugar from the work surface, then cut the marshmallow into twelve 1¾-inch squares (you'll have a bit extra). Dip the cut edges in the excess confectioners' sugar mixture on the work surface. To package, divide 1 batch among 4 bags, placing 3 marshmallows in each bag. Repeat with batches of the other variations.

Marshmallow Variations

Decidedly mature flavors, including coffee and lavender, lend these melt-in-your-mouth delicacies a sophisticated profile. Show them to their best advantage in a simple glassine bag, tied with a length of dapper ribbon.

Peppermint Marshmallows

After completing Step 3, add **1 tsp. mint extract** and beat for 30 seconds.

Chocolate Marshmallows

Before beginning steps: In a small bowl, mix together **6 Tbsp. cocoa** and **3 Tbsp. hot water** until a smooth paste forms; set aside. In Step 1, sift **¼ cup cocoa** with confectioners' sugar and cornstarch. In Step 3, beat reserved cocoa paste into reserved gelatin mixture before adding sugar mixture.

Lavender Marshmallows

Before beginning steps: In a small saucepan over high heat, bring **1 cup water** and **2 Tbsp. lavender** to a boil. Set aside and let steep for 20 minutes. Strain and reserve liquid; discard lavender. In Step 2, substitute reserved lavender water in both instances where water is called for.

Coffee Marshmallows

Before beginning steps: In a small bowl, dissolve **6 Tbsp. instant espresso** in **1 cup boiling water**. Set aside to cool to room temperature. In Step 2, substitute reserved espresso in both instances where water is called for.

Stress Free
Sidestep the tricky traditional method of making crème brûlée and do it our way—with a microwave and an oven instead of a blowtorch.

Vanilla Crème Brûlée From Good Housekeeping
Prep 12 minutes **Cook** 38 minutes **Makes** 6 servings

- 1 **cup light cream or half-and-half**
- 1 **cup heavy or whipping cream**
- 1½ **tsp. vanilla extract**
- 5 **large egg yolks**
- ⅓ **cup granulated sugar**
- 2 **Tbsp. dark brown sugar**

1. Preheat oven to 325°F. Into 13- by 9-inch metal baking pan, pour 3½ cups hot tap water; place in oven.

2. In microwave-safe 2-cup liquid measuring cup, heat creams in microwave on Medium 5 minutes. Remove from microwave; stir in vanilla.

3. Meanwhile, in 4-cup liquid measuring cup (to make pouring easier later) or bowl, whisk egg yolks and granulated sugar until well blended. Slowly whisk in warm cream until combined; with spoon, skim off foam.

4. Partially pull out oven rack with baking pan. Place six 4-ounce ramekins in water in pan in oven. Pour cream mixture into ramekins. (Mixture should come almost to tops of ramekins for successful broiling later.) Carefully push in rack and bake custards 30 minutes or until just set but centers jiggle slightly. Remove ramekins from water and place on wire rack; cool 30 minutes. Cover and refrigerate until custards are well chilled, at least 4 hours or overnight.

5. Up to 1 hour before serving, preheat broiler. Place brown sugar in coarse sieve; with spoon, press sugar through sieve to evenly cover tops of chilled custards. Place ramekins in jelly-roll pan for easier handling. With broiler rack at closest position to source of heat, broil custards 2 to 3 minutes or just until brown sugar melts. Refrigerate immediately 1 hour to cool custards and allow sugar to form a crust.

Sweet Stuff

You can make dulce de leche, a thick caramel-like sauce popular in Latin America, by boiling milk, sugar, and vanilla. Or, look for it in the canned-milk aisle at the supermarket.

Dulce de Leche Christmas Wreath

From Good Housekeeping **Prep** 35 minutes **Cook** 1 hour 10 minutes **Makes** 12 servings

- **1½ cups sliced almonds**
- **½ cup butter or margarine (1 stick)**
- **1 cup water**
- **¼ tsp. salt**
- **1 cup all-purpose flour**
- **4 large eggs, at room temperature**
- **1 cup heavy or whipping cream**
- **1 can (13.4 oz.) dulce de leche (1¼ cup)**
- **2 Tbsp. confectioners' sugar**
  Raspberries and fresh mint leaves for garnish

1. Preheat oven to 425°F. Line large cookie sheet with parchment paper. Using 8-inch plate or cake pan as guide, with nontoxic pen, trace circle on parchment. (If not using nontoxic pen, flip parchment over so that ink does not touch food.) On 15½- by 10½-inch jelly-roll pan, spread almonds in single layer. Toast 4 to 5 minutes or until golden brown, stirring occasionally. Cool almonds in pan on wire rack.

2. In 3-quart saucepan, heat butter, water, and salt to boiling on medium-high. Reduce heat to medium-low and add flour. Stir continuously 1 minute or until mixture leaves side of pan and forms a ball. Continue stirring 2 to 3 minutes or until mixture begins to coat bottom of pan. Transfer to large mixer bowl and cool 2 minutes.

3. With mixer on medium speed, beat mixture 1 minute. Continue beating and add eggs, one at a time, then beat 2 to 3 minutes longer or until satiny. The mixture should still be warm and cling to the side of the bowl. Transfer dough to large piping bag fitted with ¾-inch plain tip or to large self-sealing plastic bag with 1 corner cut to form ¾-inch hole.

4. Using circle traced on parchment as guide, pipe dough onto parchment on cookie sheet in 1-inch-thick ring just inside circle. Pipe second ring inside of first, making sure dough rings touch.

With remaining dough, pipe third ring on top of center seam of first 2 rings. With moistened finger, gently smooth dough rings where ends meet.

5. Bake 20 minutes. Reset oven control to 375°F. and bake 25 minutes or until golden. Remove wreath from oven; with tip of small knife, make several small slits all over to release steam. Bake 10 minutes longer. Cool wreath completely on cookie sheet on wire rack.

6. While wreath is cooling, whisk cream until soft peaks form. In large bowl, with mixer or wooden spoon, beat dulce de leche 5 minutes or until soft. Gently fold almonds into dulce de leche. With long serrated knife, slice wreath horizontally in half; remove and discard moist dough from inside. With spoon or spatula, spread almond mixture into bottom of wreath; top with whipped cream. Replace top of wreath.

7. To serve, dust wreath with confectioners' sugar and garnish with raspberries and mint leaves.

Healthy Eggnog

From Good Housekeeping
Prep 5 minutes plus chilling **Cook** 15 minutes
Makes 13 servings

In bowl, with whisk, beat 3 large **eggs** and 3 large **egg whites** until blended; set aside. In heavy 4-quart saucepan, with heat-safe spatula, mix 4 cups **milk** with ½ cup **sugar**, 2 Tbsp. **cornstarch**, and ¼ tsp. **salt**. Cook on medium-high until mixture boils and thickens slightly, stirring constantly. Boil 1 minute. Remove saucepan from heat. Gradually whisk ½ cup simmering milk mixture into eggs; pour egg mixture back into milk in saucepan, whisking constantly, to make custard. Pour custard into large bowl; stir in 2 Tbsp. **vanilla**, ½ tsp. **ground nutmeg**, and remaining 1½ cups **milk**. Cover and refrigerate until eggnog is well chilled, at least 6 hours or up to 2 days.

Presents
to Make and Bake

Whether you're a little bit crafty, a lot, or not, you'll find
imaginative ideas for everyone on your list

Pillow Talk

Upgrade store-bought throw pillows in a jiffy with simple appliqués.

1. To make them, type J-O-Y into a word-processing document, using a font you like. Enlarge each character to full letter-page size. Print, then cut out the letters and trace them onto white felt; cut out.

2. Next, pin strips of fusible bonding web to the back of each felt letter. Center each one (with webbing underneath) on a pillowcase and carefully remove the pins.

3. Iron on the letters according to the package instructions on the webbing. Once the letters have adhered, add decorative stitching with embroidery thread, if desired.

Oh-Sew-
Simple

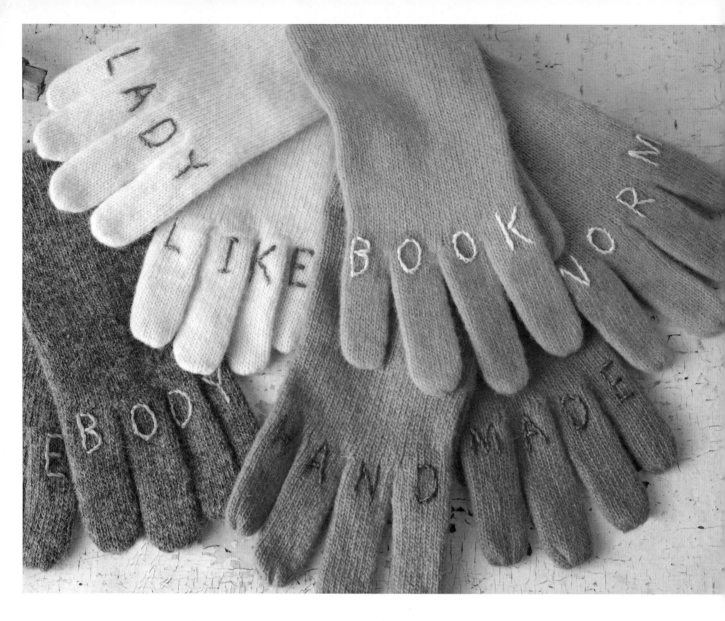

Smart stitchery lets fingers do the talking

Bring a bit of earnest irony to a pair of gloves with this hilariously tender riff on tough knuckle tattoos. Borrow our intentionally sweet phrases above, or come up with your own eight-letter expressions. We chose wool-blend gloves, but any knit version will work.

STEP ONE Slide one glove onto your hand. Using a pastel chalk pencil, mark each knuckle with a horizontal line at the bottom of each finger (the first joint) and another just below the second joint. Remove the glove, then repeat for the other hand. If needed, enlist a friend to mark your dominant hand.

STEP TWO Lay the gloves, marked sides up, on a flat surface. Working within the horizontal lines, and using the chalk pencil, spell out the phrase you plan to stitch across both gloves. Try the gloves on to check that your letters are positioned to satisfaction.

STEP THREE Using six-strand embroidery thread that contrasts with the color of your gloves, sew directly over the chalk letters with a basic stem stitch, making sure to sew through the top layer only. Remove any stray chalk with a damp cotton swab—and spread the word!

Raise the bar on the art of soap-making

A goat's-milk formula and a beguiling bird mold—along with thoughtful packaging—result in bars that seem like they cost a fortune. First, melt the soap according to package instructions. Pour the mixture into the silicone mold. Let it set for four hours, then pop out your bar. To wrap these soaps, we used unbleached coffee filters, rectangular cardboard boxes, and paper color-copied from a vintage bird guide.

Enclose each oval soap in a coffee filter before boxing— the ruffles gather neatly around curves.

Get Crafty!

Matchbox Advent Calendar ▶

Craft an Advent calendar that really stacks up.

1. Use 25 ordinary matchboxes to count down the days till Christmas.

2. Hot-glue the tops of empty boxes to one another to form rows (start with nine boxes for the base, and decrease by two until you have a single box for the top).

2. Cut wrapping paper to cover each section; secure with hot glue.

3. Next, hot-glue the rows in a pyramid shape as shown. Use number stamps (available at the crafts store) to mark the boxes 1 through 25, then fill with candy and trinkets.

Countdown made Easy!

Snowflakes

Whether you want to make the pillows or the stockings, start by creating snowflakes. Find a template online or at a crafts store. To make the pillows, trace a snowflake pattern in the center of one square of white felt (see directions at right) and cut it out. For the stockings, trace pattern onto pieces of blue and white felt and cut out.

Snowflake Pillows ▶

1. Cut two equal-sized squares in blue felt, and two in white.

2. In contrasting felt, cut one square that is ¼ inch larger all around.

3. Insert the larger white square between the two blue ones, and the larger blue square between the two white ones (the contrasting felt will make the snowflake motif pop).

4. Stitch, leaving an opening. Stuff with batting; sew shut.

5. Position white snowflake on blue felt and affix with glue or slip stitches at each point.

◀ Snowflake Stockings

1. Cut two stocking silhouettes from blue and white felt.

2. Sew together; turn inside out. Attach contrasting cuff at top.

3. Position snowflake on stocking and affix with glue or slip stitches.

Wrap It Up!

Stamps, greenery, and holiday decorations go way beyond ordinary wrapping paper and ribbon

▲ Add a Natural Accent

Thin a tablespoon of **Elmer's glue** with a small amount of **water** until it has the consistency of paint. Brush glue onto **pinecones** and **acorn tops**, then dip them in **glitter**. Let dry 5 to 10 minutes on **wax paper**. Using a **hot glue gun**, attach pinecones, acorns, and branches (snip some off your Christmas tree or buy glittered foliage at a craft store) to your present.

▲ Make Custom Gift Tags

Personalized gift tags add another fun layer to any present. Using a color copier, shrink a favorite **photo** by 50 percent to 70 percent (depending on how big a tag you want). Using **scissors**, cut out the reduced image, punch a hole in one corner, add your message on the back, and fasten to the present. You can also transform plain shipping tags—we got ours from Staples—with decorative **stamps** and **ribbons**.

Light Touch ▶

Accent packages with colorful Christmas tree light bulbs: Hot-glue six bulbs together to form a star shape, then fasten the bauble to a length of ribbon with doublestick tape. Glowing smiles guaranteed.

Create a Band of Color

1. Using **scissors**, cut a wide strip of **solid matte gift wrap** (matte paper absorbs stamp ink and dries quickly) about 2 inches shorter than the width of the box (you want to leave 1 inch on either side).

2. Wrap paper around the center of the box and fasten with tape, then cut a narrower band and tape that on top. Embellish the narrower band by decorating it with holiday-themed **stamps**.

3. For friends and family members who are high on your gift-giving list, consider getting a stamp custom-made with their name on it from your local stamp store—you can use it for years to come.

Have
Fun!

Chocolate-Dipped Pretzels

Total time 20 minutes plus chilling
Makes 27 pretzels

Place 8 oz. **milk chocolate**, broken into pieces in microwave-safe 1-cup measuring cup or mug. Heat, covered with waxed paper, in microwave on High 1 to 2 minutes or until chocolate is almost melted, stirring occasionally until smooth. Meanwhile, place **flaked coconut** and/or green, red, and white **sprinkles** on separate sheet of waxed paper or on individual plates. Using 27 8-inch-long **pretzel rods** (10 oz. bag), hold 1 pretzel rod at a time, dip in melted chocolate, tipping cup to cover about half of rod with chocolate. Allow excess chocolate to drip off pretzel back into cup. Immediately sprinkle coated pretzel with choice of topping. Carefully place coated pretzel rod in pie plate or shallow bowl, leaning uncoated portion on edge. Repeat with remaining pretzels (try to keep pretzels from touching one another in pie plate), and refrigerate about 20 minutes to set coating. Store pretzels in tightly sealed container, with waxed paper between layers, at room temperature up to 1 week.

Mini Gingerbreads

Prep 25 minutes **Cook** 35 minutes **Makes** 5 gingerbreads

- 2 **cups all-purpose flour**
- 1½ **tsp. each ground cinnamon and ground ginger**
- 1 **tsp. baking soda**
- ½ **tsp. salt**
- ½ **cup (1 stick) unsalted butter**
- 1 **cup molasses**
- ¾ **cup packed dark brown sugar**
- 2 **tsp. grated, peeled fresh ginger**
- ¾ **cup milk**
- 2 **large eggs**
- 1¼ **cups confectioners' sugar, sifted**
- 2 **Tbsp. fresh lemon juice**
- ½ **tsp. grated lemon zest**
- 2 **Tbsp. finely chopped crystallized ginger (optional)**

1. Heat oven to 350°F. Spray 5 (5¾- by 3¼- by 2-inch) foil mini loaf pans with nonstick baking spray. In a medium bowl, mix flour, cinnamon, ground ginger, baking soda, and salt.

2. In a 3-quart saucepan, melt butter over medium heat. Add molasses, brown sugar, and fresh ginger. Cook 1 minute, stirring constantly. Remove from heat. Whisk in milk and eggs. Whisk in flour mixture until batter is smooth. Pour batter into prepared pans, dividing evenly, filling pans about two-thirds full. Place loaf pans on a jelly-roll pan.

3. Bake 25 to 30 minutes, until a toothpick inserted in centers comes out clean. Cool in pans on wire rack.

4. In small bowl, whisk confectioners' sugar, lemon juice, and zest until smooth. Spoon glaze over tops of breads, spreading evenly. Sprinkle with crystallized ginger, if desired. Let glaze set.

Curried Lentil Soup Mix

Prep 5 minutes **Makes** 2 jars soup mix

- 2 (1-quart) jars with tight-fitting lids
- 1 lb. red lentils
  Salt
- 6 Tbsp. minced dried onion
- 2 Tbsp. curry powder
- 1 tsp. garlic powder
- 1 lb. green lentils
- ½ (5-oz.) pkg. dried apple rings, cut into ½-inch pieces (1 cup)
- 2 Tbsp. dried parsley leaves

1. In bottom of each glass jar, place 8 oz. red lentils; top with 1½ tsp. salt, 3 Tbsp. dried onion, 1 Tbsp. curry powder, ½ tsp. garlic powder, 8 oz. green lentils, ½ cup dried apple pieces, and 1 Tbsp. parsley, in that order. Seal jars and store at room temperature up to 1 month.

2. Prepare labels with cooking instructions; attach to jars.

NOTE: Write these cooking directions on a label and attach to jar before giving as a gift: Place soup mix in 4-quart saucepan with 7 cups water. Heat to boiling on high. Reduce heat to low; cover and simmer 20 to 30 minutes, stirring occasionally. Makes 8 cups soup.

Shred old newspapers
or book pages for inexpensive, earth-
friendly packing materials.

Porcini Salt

Smoked Paprika
& Ancho Salt

Lime-Ginger Salt

Herbes de Provence Sal

Flavored Salts

Prep 20 minutes plus drying
Makes 4 tins of 6 jars (4 of each flavor)
For each of the methods below, divide the finished salt among 4 two-ounce jars, and tighten lids to seal.
To package, fill 4 tins with shredded paper; in each tin, nestle 6 jars of salt (one of each flavor).

Porcini Salt

Using a spice grinder, and working in batches if necessary, pulse 4 ounces dried porcini mushrooms until finely ground. In a medium bowl, combine ground porcini and 1 cup fine sea salt.

Lime-Ginger Salt

Spread zest of 6 limes (about ½ cup) on waxed paper; let dry overnight. In a medium bowl, combine lime zest, 3 tsp. ground ginger, and 1 cup fine sea salt.

Smoked Paprika & Ancho Salt

Remove stems and seeds of 4 dried ancho chiles. Using a mortar and pestle, break up chiles. Using a spice grinder, and working in batches if necessary, pulse until coarsely ground. In a medium bowl, combine ground chiles, ¼ cup smoked paprika, and ¾ cup fine sea salt.

Herbes de Provence Salt

Using a spice grinder, and working in batches if necessary, pulse ½ cup herbes de Provence and 6 Tbsp. dried lavender until coarsely ground. In a medium bowl, combine ground herbes de Provence and lavender and ¾ cup fine sea salt.

Celery Salt

Preheat oven to 250°F. Place leaves from 4 heads of celery on 2 parchment-lined baking pans and bake until dry, about 10 minutes. Let cool completely. Using a spice grinder, and working in batches if necessary, pulse until coarsely ground. In a medium bowl, combine ground celery leaves and 1 cup fine sea salt.

Curry Salt

Using a mortar and pestle, crush 12 medium dried bay leaves until coarsely ground. In a medium bowl, combine ground bay leaves with ¼ cup garam masala, ¼ cup curry powder, 2 tsp. ground cumin, and ½ cup fine sea salt.

Gingerbread Cookie Puzzles

Prep 45 minutes **Cook** 20 minutes **Makes** eight 4- by 6-inch puzzles

In a large bowl, combine 2½ cups all-purpose **flour**, 1 Tbsp. **ground ginger**, ½ tsp. **ground cloves**, and ¼ tsp. **salt** and set aside. In a medium saucepan on medium, place 1 stick **unsalted butter**, ½ cup **dark corn syrup**, ¼ cup **dark-brown sugar**, and ¼ cup **granulated sugar**, and cook until butter melts and sugars dissolve. Add butter mixture to flour mixture, and stir with a wooden spoon until combined. Divide dough in half and cover in plastic wrap; pat into ½-inch-thick squares. Chill until very firm, 4 hours or overnight, then follow directions below.

THE KEY TO THIS PUZZLING PASTRY?

1. First, roll out dough on a well-floured surface to ⅛ inch thick. Cut out eight 4- by 6-inch rectangles.

2. Working with 1 rectangle at a time (keep others in fridge), use a 2½-inch-tall cookie cutter to punch out a gingerbread boy from center.

3. With a paring knife, cut 8 to 12 pieces from around gingerbread boy to create a puzzle, as shown.

4. Using a spatula, transfer pieces to a parchment-lined baking sheet and refrigerate for 20 minutes.

5. Repeat with remaining rectangles.

6. Preheat oven to 350°F. Remove puzzles from refrigerator and use a knife to gently separate cutout pieces from one another (about ½ inch) so that they don't fuse in the oven.

7. Brush gingerbread boy lightly with beaten egg white and sprinkle with sugar. Bake 12 minutes. Let cool completely.

8. Place cooled cookie puzzles in boxes to give as gifts.

Vanilla Caramels

Prep 45 minutes **Cook** 30 minutes **Makes** 60 pieces

> Vegetable oil, for greasing
> 1   cup sugar
> 1   cup heavy cream
> ½   cup unsalted butter
> 1   cup light corn syrup
> 1½ tsp. vanilla extract

1. Line an 8-inch-square pan with foil and generously brush with vegetable oil. Set aside.

2. In a medium saucepan on high, cook sugar, without stirring, until it begins to melt and bubble. Using a metal spoon, stir slowly until sugar has completely melted, about 1 minute. Remove from heat and add cream (sugar will seize into a solid mass). Add butter and corn syrup.

3. Fit a candy thermometer to saucepan, return to stovetop, and cook over low heat, stirring occasionally until mixture liquefies, about 30 minutes. Increase heat to medium-high, and cook until caramel mixture reaches 238°F. Remove pan from heat; stir in vanilla extract.

4. Carefully pour caramel into prepared pan. Using a spatula coated in vegetable oil, smooth any bubbles on surface. Cool caramel until firm but still slightly warm, about 35 minutes.

5. Lift caramel from pan and peel away foil. Place on an oiled cutting board and cut into 1-inch squares, using an oiled knife.

6. Wrap each cooled candy in waxed paper.

Butter-Crunch Toffee

Prep 20 minutes **Cook** 20 minutes **Makes** 1½ lbs.

> 1   cup slivered almonds, toasted
> 1   cup (2 sticks) unsalted butter
> 1   cup sugar
> 3   Tbsp. water
> 1   Tbsp. corn syrup (light or dark)
> ¼   tsp. salt
> 6   oz. bittersweet or semisweet chocolate, finely chopped

1. Line a 13- by 9- by 2-inch baking pan with foil, extending foil over ends of pan. Sprinkle ½ cup of the almonds in pan. Finely chop the remaining ½ cup nuts.

2. Butter sides of a heavy 2-quart saucepan. In saucepan, melt butter. Add sugar, water, corn syrup, and salt. Cook, stirring, on medium-high until mixture boils. Insert a candy thermometer. Reduce heat to medium and boil mixture, stirring frequently, until candy thermometer registers 290°F. (soft-crack stage). After mixture reaches 280°F., stir and watch carefully to prevent scorching. Remove saucepan from heat; remove thermometer and pour candy over almonds in pan.

3. Let stand 5 minutes; sprinkle with chocolate. Let stand until chocolate softens, about 2 minutes. Spread chocolate evenly over candy. Sprinkle with chopped almonds. Refrigerate candy until firm. Use foil to lift candy from pan; break into pieces. Store tightly covered at room temperature.

Bark if you love chocolate

Coworkers, bosses—heck, we'll wager even the mailman will devour this D.I.Y. candy. Double the recipe and give it to everyone.

Prep 20 minutes plus chilling **Makes** 1–1 ½ lbs.

Chocolate peppermint bark

12 oz. bittersweet or semisweet chocolate, chopped
½ cup coarsely crushed red peppermint candies

1. Line a baking sheet with nonstick foil or parchment.
2. Melt chocolate in a microwave-safe bowl on high for 1 minute. Remove from microwave and stir. Heat 15 to 30 seconds more. Stir until smooth.
3. Pour chocolate onto prepared baking sheet and spread into a ¼-inch-thick rectangle using a metal spatula. Sprinkle with crushed peppermint.
4. Refrigerate 1 hour or until firm. Peel off foil and break bark into pieces. It will keep about one month in an airtight container in refrigerator.

Chocolate marble bark

12 oz. bittersweet or semisweet chocolate, chopped
 3 oz. white chocolate, chopped
½ cup each pecans and slivered almonds, toasted

1. Repeat step 1 in first recipe.
2. Repeat step 2 in first recipe to melt bittersweet chocolate.
3. For white chocolate: In a separate bowl, melt on medium for 30 seconds. Stir and heat again for 30 seconds. Stir and repeat 2 more times, 30 seconds each, until white chocolate is smooth.
4. Pour dark chocolate onto prepared baking sheet as in first recipe. Drop dollops of white chocolate on top of dark chocolate. Draw a skewer or a thin knife through chocolates to marble. Sprinkle with pecans and almonds.
5. Repeat step 4 in first recipe.

Salty, sweet,
nutty, fruity—the bark
options are endless!

Pistachio cranberry white-chocolate bark

12 oz. white chocolate, chopped
¾ cup each shelled pistachio nuts and dried cranberries

1. Repeat step 1 in first recipe.
2. Repeat step 3 in second recipe to melt white chocolate.
3. Repeat step 3 in first recipe, but sprinkle with pistachios and cranberries.
4. Repeat step 4 in first recipe.

Tropical white-chocolate bark

12 oz. white chocolate, chopped
¼ cup each chopped dried papaya and pineapple
½ cup coconut flakes, toasted
½ cup macadamia nuts, toasted

1. Repeat step 1 in first recipe.
2. Repeat step 3 in second recipe to melt white chocolate.
3. Repeat step 3 in first recipe, but sprinkle with papaya, pineapple, coconut, and macadamia nuts.
4. Repeat step 4 in first recipe.

Movie-night bark

12 oz. milk chocolate, chopped
½ cup mini pretzels, broken
½ cup Cracker Jack mix, Poppycock, or caramel popcorn
½ cup salted peanuts
½ cup chocolate-covered raisins (halved if large)

1. Repeat step 1 in first recipe.
2. Repeat step 2 in first recipe to melt milk chocolate.
3. Repeat step 3 in first recipe, but sprinkle with pretzels, Cracker Jack mix, peanuts, and chocolate-covered raisins.
4. Repeat step 4 in first recipe.

"Christmas waves a magic wand over this world, and behold, everything is softer and more beautiful."

— **Norman Vincent Peale**

Index

Note: Page numbers in *italics* indicate photos on pages other than recipes or main discussions.

Photography Credits

Antonis Achilleos: 71

Alamy: 97 (Pippin and Golden Delicious); Jiri Hera: 9; Tina Rupp: 22

Sang An: 12 bottom

Michel Arnaud: 38, 39 (all photos), 45 top and middle

James Baigrie: 5 top left, 63, 64, 65, 69 (both photos), 75, 76, 77 right, 80, 82, 83 top

Monica Buck: 8 (Brownie Bites)

Beatriz da Costa: 77 left, 90 top

Getty Images: 62, 94 bottom; Sean Justice: 20; James Jackson: 21; Jim Franco: 23 top; Michael Paul: 90 bottom

Aimée Herring: 36 (pinecone ornament), 37

IPC + Syndication: Paul Raeside/Livingetc: 54; Tim Young/Country Homes & Interiors: 55 top left; Dan Duchars/Ideal Home: 55 top right and bottom left

iStockphoto: Lauri Patterson: 107

Frances Janisch: 5 bottom left, 23 bottom left, 24, 26 bottom right, 29, 30 left, 44, 45 bottom, 56, 57 (all photos), 99, 101, 112 bottom, 113

John Kernick: 70, 73, 92

Yunhee Kim: 85, 86, 88, 94 top, 95, 96, 98

Loupe Images: Ryland Peters & Small Ltd: 48 bottom left, 50 bottom right

Rita Maas: 116 top, 121 right

Kate Mathis: 46, 48 bottom right, 55 bottom right, 59, 60, 67, 79, 87, 100, 105, 106, 116 bottom left, 117

Andrew McCaul: 5 top right, 42 bottom left, 47 bottom left, 48 top right, 114 bottom right

Ellen McDermott: 42 top left and bottom right, 51

James Merrell: 110 (both photos), 111

Ellie Miller: 3, 4 (cookies), 14, 15, 16, 18-19

Ngoc Minh Ngo: 91

Helen Norman: 5 bottom right, 47 top left

Michael Partenio: 33, 34, 35 (all photos), 40, 41 (all photos), 89

José Picayo: 104, 118

Andrew Purcell: 122-123

Tina Rupp: 12 top, 13, 26 top, 27, 30 right, 31, 103

Hector Sanchez: 83 bottom

Charles Schiller: 42 top right

Victor Schrager: 36 (all except pinecones), 50 left, 112 top, 124

Kate Sears: 7, 8 (Gingersnaps and Linzer), 11

Shutterstock: 97 (Granny Smith)

Ellen Silverman: 49

Ann Stratton: 74, 78, 102

Studio D: Philip Friedman: 50 top right, 93; Lara Robby: 52-53, 109, 114 top left and right, 115, 120, 121 left

U.S. Apple Association: 97 (Cameo, Jonathan, Rome Beauty)

Jonny Valiant: 4 left, 43, 68, 72, 81 (both photos)

Björn Wallander: 48 top left

Wendell T. Weber: 47 right

Front Cover: Ellie Miller

Back Cover: Jonny Valiant

Front Flap: Sang An

Back Flap: Ellie Miller

HEARST BOOKS

New York

An Imprint of Sterling Publishing
387 Park Avenue South
New York, NY 10016

ISBN 978-1-61837-143-0

Distributed in Canada by Sterling Publishing
c/o Canadian Manda Group, 165 Dufferin Street
Toronto, Ontario, Canada M6K 3H6

Distributed in the United Kingdom by GMC Distribution Services
Castle Place, 166 High Street, Lewes, East Sussex, England BN7 1XU

Distributed in Australia by Capricorn Link (Australia) Pty. Ltd.
P.O. Box 704, Windsor, NSW 2756, Australia

For information about custom editions, special sales, and premium and corporate purchases,
please contact Sterling Special Sales at 800-805-5489 or specialsales@sterlingpublishing.com.

Manufactured in China

2 4 6 8 10 9 7 5 3 1

www.sterlingpublishing.com